1,000,000 Books

are available to read at

www.ForgottenBooks.com

Read online
Download PDF
Purchase in print

ISBN 978-0-282-38758-7
PIBN 10849996

This book is a reproduction of an important historical work. Forgotten Books uses state-of-the-art technology to digitally reconstruct the work, preserving the original format whilst repairing imperfections present in the aged copy. In rare cases, an imperfection in the original, such as a blemish or missing page, may be replicated in our edition. We do, however, repair the vast majority of imperfections successfully; any imperfections that remain are intentionally left to preserve the state of such historical works.

Forgotten Books is a registered trademark of FB &c Ltd.
Copyright © 2018 FB &c Ltd.
FB &c Ltd, Dalton House, 60 Windsor Avenue, London, SW19 2RR.
Company number 08720141. Registered in England and Wales.

For support please visit www.forgottenbooks.com

1 MONTH OF FREE READING

at
www.ForgottenBooks.com

By purchasing this book you are eligible for one month membership to ForgottenBooks.com, giving you unlimited access to our entire collection of over 1,000,000 titles via our web site and mobile apps.

To claim your free month visit: www.forgottenbooks.com/free849996

* Offer is valid for 45 days from date of purchase. Terms and conditions apply.

English
Français
Deutsche
Italiano
Español
Português

www.forgottenbooks.com

Mythology Photography **Fiction** Fishing Christianity **Art** Cooking Essays Buddhism Freemasonry Medicine **Biology** Music **Ancient Egypt** Evolution Carpentry Physics Dance Geology **Mathematics** Fitness Shakespeare **Folklore** Yoga Marketing **Confidence** Immortality Biographies Poetry **Psychology** Witchcraft Electronics Chemistry History **Law** Accounting **Philosophy** Anthropology Alchemy Drama Quantum Mechanics Atheism Sexual Health **Ancient History Entrepreneurship** Languages Sport Paleontology Needlework Islam **Metaphysics** Investment Archaeology Parenting Statistics Criminology **Motivational**

LIBRARY
Connecticut Agricultural

Vol.	28/67
Class	640
Cost	G.H.
Date	Sept, 12

Please
handle this volume
with care.

The University of Connecticut
Libraries, Storrs

3 9153 01301626 8

This Book may be kept out

TWO WEEKS

only and is subject to a fine of TWO CENTS a day thereafter. It will be due on the day indicated below.

GOOD HOUSEKEEPING'S
Book on
THE BUSINESS OF HOUSEKEEPING

A Manual of Method

By
Mildred Maddocks Bentley
Home Economics: Consultant and Writer

*New Ways of Handling the
Familiar Routine of Housework*

Published by GOOD HOUSEKEEPING
119 West Fortieth Street, New York

Copyright, 1924, by
GOOD HOUSEKEEPING MAGAZINE
INTERNATIONAL MAGAZINE COMPANY, INC.

All rights reserved, including that of translation
into foreign languages, including
the Scandinavian

28/67

FIRST PRINTING
October, 1924
SECOND PRINTING
March, 1925

Printed in the United States of America by
J. J. LITTLE AND IVES COMPANY, NEW YORK

Foreword

THE good housekeeper must bring to her task of housekeeping every one of the qualities that make for a successful executive in the downtown business world. She must be able to handle people—I know of no employees more difficult than the green maid of all work, the temperamental couple, or the casual by-the-day worker. She must be able to buy wisely—and her purchases total an aggregate in most families of from 50 to 75% of the total income enjoyed.

Finally, she must know the actual processes involved in her business of housekeeping much as her husband knows factory methods lying back of the product he must market. Heretofore this housekeeping lore was handed down from mother to daughter, but today such an equipment for her new business is not enough for the young housewife. Methods and appliances have improved so tremendously that the new housekeeping bears little relation to the old task. Both mechanical and chemical assistants are replacing much of the old hard hand drudgery.

For some sixteen years Good Housekeeping Institute has been testing out new appliances and new housekeeping methods. This volume represents the results of some of this research work. It has had the further proof of actual operation in the home of the writer—an average home with all of the every day problems that the average American home must meet. I feel confident that in offering you this manual of method Good Housekeeping is filling a long felt want on the library shelf of progressive housekeepers.

MILDRED MADDOCKS BENTLEY

Contents

	PAGE
FOREWORD	5

SECTION I.—THE NEW HOUSEKEEPING

CHAPTER
I.	LABOR-SAVING EQUIPMENT	11
II.	A CALL TO BUDGETING	17

SECTION II.—SERVANTS AND HOUSE-KEEPERS

I.	THE SINGLE MAID RÉGIME	29
II.	THE ROUTINE OF TWO SERVANTS	34

SECTION III.—ROUTINE HOUSEHOLD TASKS

I.	THE DAILY ROUTINE OF DOWNSTAIRS CARE .	43
II.	THE DAILY ROUTINE OF UPSTAIRS CARE . .	50
III.	DISHWASHING THREE TIMES A DAY . . .	60
IV.	THE CARE OF THE REFRIGERATOR	67

SECTION IV.—SPECIAL HOUSEHOLD TASKS

I.	SILVER CLEANING	73
II.	METAL CLEANING	78

CONTENTS

CHAPTER		PAGE
III.	FLOOR TREATMENT AND CARE	84
IV.	FURNITURE CLEANING AND POLISHING	95
V.	CLOSET AND STOREROOM CARE	100
VI.	CELLAR CARE AND CLEANLINESS	106
VII.	SPRING RENOVATING	110
VIII.	SEASONAL HOUSE CLEANING	116
IX.	SAFE PROCEDURE IN CLOSING A HOUSE	120

SECTION V.—IN THE LAUNDRY

I.	PLAN AND LOCATION	129
II.	EQUIPMENT, CHOICE AND INSTALLATION	134
III.	WASHING FORMULAS	147

    Soaps and Soap Compounds
    Softeners
    Blues and Tints
    Lingerie Tints and Dyes
    Starches and Starching

IV.	LAUNDRY METHODS	160

    The Chemistry of Washing
    The Routine of the Family Wash
    The Removal of Stains
    Sprinkling and Folding
    Washing Silks and Woolens
    Fitting the Baby's Wash into
      the House Routine

SECTION I

The New Housekeeping

Chapter I—Labor-Saving Equipment

Chapter II—A Call to Budgeting

CHAPTER I

Labor-Saving Equipment

THE new housekeeping is vastly different from the old régime. Largely because well made, efficient machines replace much of the hand labor of our grandmother's time, the modern beginner in household lore must learn a new system of planning and new methods of work.

Many are at a loss to decide just what machines are the indispensable ones for their housework and put off acquiring any because of this uncertainty. Frankly there is ample opportunity for saving both time and labor as well as money in servant hire by the purchase of well constructed and well designed equipment. And it is a fallacy to think that servants cannot learn to use them.

For instance, for the kitchen there are today **well planned kitchen cabinet** systems either in wood or metal to take the place of the large pantries and to accomplish their work better. This same new housekeeper has her choice of gas or electric ranges with heat regulated ovens, electric

BUSINESS OF HOUSEKEEPING

fireless cookers and fireless cookers to be used in conjunction with the gas range; pressure cookers and ranges burning oil so efficiently that this quick fuel has revolutionized the country kitchen. There is something for every one of you.

Water heating systems enable her to have an ample supply of hot water at temperatures high enough for the best work, and she can select her fuel—gas, oil, or electricity in the few sections its cost would not make it prohibitive.

Electric refrigeration is more than a dream. It is a real fact of accomplishment. In the larger sizes (250 pounds ice capacity) refrigerators are less costly to operate than with ice service even at high rates for electricity and in both large and small sizes they furnish lower refrigeration and better food conservation with some additional saving in time and labor hitherto involved in cleaning the refrigerator. When the first cost can be assumed they prove indispensable in the well ordered home.

The single piece double **drainboard sink,** set high—from 34 to 36 inches from the floor to bottom of sink—has worked wonders as a real labor saver. **A dishwasher** installed to waste and supply as a pantry sink saves both drudgery and hands.

In a single maid household it enables daughter or mother to care for all serving dishes; leaving the cooking dishes to be washed at the kitchen sink by the maid.

LABOR SAVING EQUIPMENT

Even the **linoleum**, cemented to the kitchen floor, proves an appreciable labor saver in that it eliminates floor scrubbing and reduces the care to a semi-weekly or weekly cleaning and polishing with liquid wax, and a very occasioual mopping followed by the polishing.

Laundry equipment has revolutionized home laundering methods. The indispensables are a washing machine, an ironing machine and a dryer for use on stormy days. The latter however should not take the place of all the "sun and air" drying the weatherman allows to the housekeeper. Ceiling dryer racks are convenient as are also low benches on casters for easy rolling. A well designed wall-hung ironing board for hand work with electric irons of different weights should be provided. Not until one really stops to think, is it possible to realize what these mean as work-savers in comparison with the hand washing methods, the hand wringer and the old-fashioned sad irons.

The **vacuum cleaner** and the **electric sewing machine** stand out as indispensable equipment for their several tasks. Tribute must also be paid to the chemically prepared and the wax and oil treated mops, dusters and polishing cloths. These save more work than one credits at first thought, because they have revolutionized floor, wood trim and furniture care.

Space does not permit mention of all the excellent special devices for a kitchen, laundry, etc. Sufficient to say there

BUSINESS OF HOUSEKEEPING

are few household tasks that are not helped by some machine worthy to purchase, provided the task that they care for is sufficiently routine to warrant the original outlay.

Just a word as to what shall govern your selection. Choose all household equipment from the tested and approved lists of Good Housekeeping Institute. Look for the seal of approval. Any device so listed is a safe purchase and you can be saved untold annoyance and dissatisfaction by selecting a machine that prolonged test has proved to be well made and efficient. In practically no instance is there any single "best." Like automobiles of similar price class there are varieties of appeal that, quite aside from quality, affect the purchaser's decision. More important, I believe, than any consideration other than quality is a choice that secures dealer interest and knowledge of the device, with ability to replace minor parts promptly. Give the preference, then, to a device handled in your locality.

In conclusion just a word as to financing the purchase of household equipment. While there is a saving in an outright purchase, there are nevertheless many women with housekeeping allowances liberal enough to provide for regular monthly payments if these could be saved out of the wages of day workers or other servant hire. But "installment plan" buying has a bad name among these housekeepers and they do not take advantage of the method because they fail to distinguish between investing in machines that work out their own payment and assuming the long time purchase of a luxury whose entire cost it would be impossible to meet. At present much household equipment involving power can be purchased through the local power company to be paid for by a series of monthly payments added to the gas or electric bill. It is a method that commends itself to the thoughtful housekeeper who otherwise might have to defer her investment.

SCIENTIFIC HOUSEKEEPING

I have recently read several books on the subject of scientific management in connection with my industrial work, and I began to apply the principles to my household tasks. I started with dishwashing, studying my present practise, utensils, motions, sequences of motions, etc., with the purpose of forming a standard practise. I expected to be surprised, but the results amazed me, not only that so much time was saved, but that I found how much I was enjoying the work.—*Good Housekeeping Discovery.*

CONSERVING ONE'S STRENGTH

This suggestion from a physician may be of value in conserving the strength of other housewives. "Never lift anything with the back bent; learn to crouch down and lift with a straight spine, making the weight come on the arms. Many a tired or sprained back could be avoided in this way." —*Good Housekeeping Discovery.*

BUSINESS OF HOUSEKEEPING

FOR SUNDAY MORNING

We are all doubtless familiar with households where every member seems to feel grumpy on Sunday morning—grown-ups because they wanted to sleep and couldn't because the children made so much noise, and the children cross because they were hungry and breakfast was a little late. I know a home where this problem has been met to every one's satisfaction for years. Saturday night mother places by the side of the children's beds a small piece of bread and butter, or plain coffee cake, and a bit of fruit, only a small piece. The piece is wrapped carefully in waxed paper and is not enough to interfere with appetites for breakfast. And it is such fun to wake up and see "what mother brought up this morning." That extra half-hour nap is a luxury for the rest of the family, the kiddies are happy, and the day starts right.

—*Good Housekeeping Discovery.*

SAFETY FIRST

For the sake of a healthier town in which to live, faithfully promise yourself that you will make a hole in every tin can that you dispose of. It takes only a moment, and yet it effectually prevents stagnant water collecting —the sure breeding place for mosquitoes. Never mind what other people do, your conscience will be clear, and perhaps you can induce others to follow your example.

—*Good Housekeeping Discovery.*

CHAPTER II

A Call to Budgeting

DO you run your home like a business? Do you plan your work so that a part of your twenty-four hour day belongs to you as an individual?

The stereotyped call to budgeting and account-keeping, with directions that accompany it, appeals generally to the one type of housekeeper—the mathematically-minded, who already handles figures with the alertness of familiarity and love. Perhaps because I am one of them, I believe there are hosts of other housekeepers who are terrified by digits as digits, but who can overcome this terror when their value, as a means toward system and thrift in housekeeping, is once clearly demonstrated.

Proportions are and must be flexible because of the flexible value of the dollar. But keep account of your spending under the proper headings. Plot the proportion from the charges that are fixed obligations which you must meet. It may be rent, it may be buying a home: that is your starting point. It may even be an unusual cost of sickness. But in **budgeting** it is always essential, in planning, to start from fixed obligations, molding the balance of money-spending around them. At the end of the year you will have more valuable information than you can acquire by any study of some one else's experience.

The smaller the income to be plotted, the more necessary it is that one hand shall hold the purse strings. And it is essential to pick the best financier in the family for that task, be it husband or wife. The other members of the family should not feel degraded by asking for any sum that can be expended with fairness to the income's obligations. It is all in the cause of dollar efficiency.

When the income is large enough for greater ease in living, it may well be divided for convenience in handling individual needs. The important thing is not who handles the money, but how the money is handled. When a proportion that entails a sacrifice to the balance of the family is spent upon one member's wants and wishes, then is the time for a business-like talk that will more fairly adjust the income. The point I wish to make is that allowances are not essential to fairness. They sometimes work a hardship to the small income.

The **envelope system** for paying bills is undoubtedly the simplest for the smaller salaries that are to be spent as cash. Into the several envelopes—or small boxes, if you will—place the weekly sums to be devoted to the several budget items. Into the rent envelope is tucked the week's proportion of the rent, and so with all the rest.

A CALL TO BUDGETING

Itemize your expenses down to the last detail if you enjoy bookkeeping, but it is not actually necessary for efficient budgeting. It is often valuable to know the relative expenditures for groceries, meat, milk, and fruit, because these proportions often tell a story of good or poor nourishment. It is well, then, to keep these with comparative accuracy. But to be a slave to the jotting down of the purchase of every yeast cake often discourages a housekeeper from enjoying the benefits of budgeting her income, and is not really essential.

A monthly payment system commonly called the credit system has obvious advantages. Where it is possible to deposit this house money as a checking account, to my mind it can be spent more wisely. But there are two "buts." It is only fair to the bank to give them the use of the money for at least fifteen days—a whole month is, of course, still better. By depositing your money on the fifteenth, they have this money for their own use until the third or fourth of the month, and the handling of your checks will show a slight profit and not a loss to them. If you deposit your money on the first of the month and check it out on the fourth, you can see the cost it will entail upon the bank. Many small banks will appreciably cut the sum required for deposit, if you in turn will deposit on the fifteenth money to be used after the first of the month. The second "but" is psychological. Train yourself to pay out the money mentally as you make a credit purchase. If

BUSINESS OF HOUSEKEEPING

you do this, the first of the month will bring you no surprises. You will not overdraw your account. With these two safe-guards the credit system, for even the small income, is most efficient. But you must protect your bank, and you must protect your bank-account.

Many families have found the following figures helpful. The figures are based on a family of five, and have been formulated and used by the Home Service Departments of many banks.

Monthly Income	$150.00	$200.00	$300.00	$400.00
Savings	11.00	25.00	40.00	65.00
Food	50.00	50.00	60.00	75.00
Shelter	38.00	50.00	75.00	100.00
Clothing	26.00	32.00	50.00	50.00
Operating Expense	13.00	18.00	30.00	50.00
Advancement	12.00	25.00	40.00	60.00
Monthly Income	$500.00	$600.00	$700.00	$800.00
Savings	100.00	125.00	175.00	200.00
Food	75.00	85.00	100.00	100.00
Shelter	125.00	150.00	150.00	150.00
Clothing	60.00	70.00	80.00	100.00
Operating Expense	60.00	80.00	95.00	100.00
Advancement	80.00	90.00	100.00	150.00

Lack of clear and definite standards for using the income causes much financial worry. It is not possible for the majority of people to mass great wealth and build up large estates, but when one has made a workable plan so that out of each instalment of the income he is (1) making provisions for the future, (2) building up a reserve which he can use for seasonal and large expenses, and (3) taking care of current expenses, he can at least have the satisfaction of

A CALL TO BUDGETING

knowing that he is laying the proper foundation and steering toward financial safety.

So while budgeting points out to you the way your dollars are traveling, an actual control of that dollar travel can be obtained only by careful and intelligent planning. But not until householders try it do they realize how much control they have over the situation. In one family **gas for water heating** costs $20 per month. Another family of similar size and hot water equipment has a monthly bill of only $5. In the latter case lea**ky faucets** are promptly packed, but what is even more important, each member of the household uses the hot water supply with moderation and no waste.

You can appreciably affect your **lighting bills** by supplying varied sizes of bulbs. I am taking it for granted that you turn out the lights when they are not needed, and that you renew the tungstens before they are discolored and obscure light. It is glaring illumination, not lighting for comfort or efficiency, that makes your current bills too high. Therefore, where you want a general illumination only, as in halls, closets, etc., and direct lighting overhead fixtures, use ten-watt lamps. This, of course, does not apply to any of the indirect lighting overhead fixtures. It would take five of these small lamps each burning an hour to equal the cost of your commonly used 50-watt size. For all reading lamps, wherever you need efficient lighting for work or for play, of course use the fifty or seventy-five watt lamps. Comfort is increased, and bills are decreased.

Heating leaks need a word. Save yourself coal next winter by jacketing your furnace or boiler and its conducting pipes with asbestos cement. The saving right there can run into tons of coal in a large house. It will mean a ton or more even for a small house. Install a heat regulator; you will save another ton there, for it almost takes the place of a skilled engineer, since the coal burns evenly to a fine ash. Clean and keep clean the furnace, pipes, and flues. If you have done all this, you are wasting no more fuel than you can prevent.

The leaks in buying food are many. For the small family, I have definitely proved that "shopping around" with cash may be wasteful. I am aware that this is heresy to many, but here are my reasons. The total amount of food consumed by a small number of people, two or four, carries with it a profit that is interesting enough when but one grocer and one butcher, etc., receive it, but scatter those profits, and not a tradesman is really interested in your preference. You are thrown back on your own skill in selecting the best, and one mistake means loss to you, because you cannot return the cash purchase. But even one mistake carries loss to the credit store, so that the store where you carry an account maintains the standards of quality you demand, with but few slips.

A *CALL TO BUDGETING*

Try my system when moving into a new town or neighborhood. At first shop around, paying cash, until you find the butcher, the grocer, and the vegetable man whose quality of goods suits you. Then go to the proprietor, tell him what your approximate monthly bill is to be, and state that you would be glad to promise your exclusive patronage and prompt monthly payment so long as quality and service are fair and satisfactory. I have used this same policy in managing an apartment for myself and maid, a home for a larger family, and a hospital family of two hundred and fifty. It has never failed to produce the best of treatment with real, thrift prices.

Just a word here about **telephone ordering.** It need not be an extravagant or wasteful method. If I had not consistently used it, I should never have been able to accomplish other as important tasks. In one year I visited my grocer twice. At those times he did not recognize me, but he did recognize the quality that must be delivered to that address. I am aware that this is, again, heresy. And the secret of success probably does lie in a knowledge of food values, foods in season, and food market costs. But it is a knowledge that all may acquire. Refuse to be satisfied with other than the standard you yourself have set. Send back the first wilted head of lettuce, and there will be no second. Spend fifteen minutes each week to check over the grocer's statement. How can he cheat you?

BUSINESS OF HOUSEKEEPING

Where the family is larger than the one indicated, **staple supplies** must of course be bought in quantity, for storage space then pays for itself. And in this case shopping around for both seasons and price is essential and to your advantage. But in purchasing in these large quantities do not make the mistake of using, or allowing them to be used, from the large containers. Treat the store-room as your grocery store, and keep the kitchen cabinet stocked with current supplies. Even the most intelligent of us is affected, by an abundance, to use a bit more generously than necessary, thus jeopardizing the advantage of the close buying.

Take your butcher into your confidence as you have your grocer. Let him have all your trade and know that he is going to get it just as long as he respects it. Let your saving come in the selection of cuts and a wise use of leftovers. The housekeeper who shops around for meats gets cheated nine times out of ten in quality or flavor or quantity.

TAKING ADVANTAGE OF SALES

This is my money savings plan. In the memorandum of my family account-book I have listed the various special sales of different department stores with the dates on which they fall. There are the shoe, furniture, drug, stationery, silk, underwear, and many other sales which are always

A CALL TO BUDGETING

offered during the same month in each year. On the following pages I make notes, as they occur to me, of articles which I shall need. For instance, I find that my visiting cards are nearly gone. I jot this down and, turning to my notes, I find at about what date I can have cards engraved from my plate at a saving of fifty cents per hundred. Or I wish to lay in a supply of sheets and pillowcases and take note of the month when white sales are at their best. I have practised this plan in a town of ten thousand people and in a city of nearly half a million, and I know that it works well in both places. Aside from the dollars saved by this ever-ready information, there is a great satisfaction in being able to plan my expenses in a more efficient way.

—*Good Housekeeping Discovery.*

A BUDGET HELP

In making small purchases I always plan to pay for them in bills, and in this way I am able to keep on hand about five dollars in change. This change is kept in the proper divisions of a small cash box, and when the delivery boys arrive, I am sure they bless me for being able to hand over to them the proper change without any trouble. I am sure, too, that it is a great comfort to me to have the change I need without having to borrow from a guest or a maid or even a neighbor.

—*Good Housekeeping Discovery.*

MY GOOD HOUSEKEEPING SAVINGS BANK

Last year, I kept a small bank which I called my GOOD HOUSEKEEPING bank, and into it I put all money saved by following any economical suggestion given on the Discovery page. To illustrate: I made window screens by Discovery directions instead of buying them, and put in the bank the difference in cost of making the screens and buying them. Several such instances came up, and by the end of the year I had saved enough money to give GOOD HOUSEKEEPING subscriptions to several of my friends.

—Good Housekeeping Discovery.

SECTION II

Servants and Housekeepers

Chapter I—The Single Maid Régime
Chapter II—The Routine of Two Servants

CHAPTER I

The Single Maid Régime

A MOST important factor in the smooth running of a home that is every good homemaker's aim is **system.** Whether the work is to be accomplished by paid labor or labor paid by love alone, a schedule is a help. On the other hand it is not possible to lay down any hard and fast rules because duties must vary in their relative importance with the individual requirements of each family. At the same time I believe many of us have not realized the increasing complexity of the "general housework" duties that we have been demanding from a single worker. It has been very gradually that living conditions of the average American family have been raised in so far as the refinements of living are concerned. But there is no question that these present high standards must be considered with relation to household service and that there must be some modification in our demands upon a single worker. Many housekeepers, especially those that have just assumed the duties, are uncertain just what it is fair to expect from the household workers they hire.

BUSINESS OF HOUSEKEEPING

With two only in a family I believe it is fair to look for a single maid who will cook simple meals, keep the house merely tidy, and undertake the laundry work. Or this same general maid will cook simple meals and keep the house really clean, with laundry work simplified by washing and ironing machines. At the same time, even in so small a family, the frills of service must be eliminated. For one thing waiting on table can be simplified. I know this is heresy to many housekeepers who wish things "done nicely," but a trial will prove the plan has the practical advantage of accomplishing more real housework.

Under this scheme each course is served on the table by the host or hostess and the maid is required only at the change of courses and for the replenishment of food, water, etc. The answering of bells and doors and telephone messages should be otherwise provided for, save when no member of the family is at home to respond. This plan leaves the maid free for her long stretches of work such as cleaning or washing and ironing.

In a family of three, the schedule was worked out with more than fair success by the single worker accomplishing the cooking and the care of the entire downstairs floor. She also finishes all laundry that is not completed by a single day's work per week of the laundress. The entire upstairs work is assumed by the family with what day worker help they may need for the rough cleaning. But

THE SINGLE MAID REGIME

here, too, telephone, door and table waiting has been placed on a simplified basis.

In larger families than these a single worker becomes cook only, and possibly laundress. But all other duties must be assumed by the various members of the family or by outside help. The schedules vary, you see, with practically the same work to be accomplished. I give them all to show you the difficulty of standardizing work. It is your family and your requirements and the special ability of the maid herself that must settle the kinds of work she will undertake. But remember do not attempt to make the term general houseworker elastic enough to cover all of our modern living requirements.

The actual weekly schedule can well be applied to a housekeeper herself or to the single maid. It is affected vitally by the consideration of equipment. In the household provided with a **washing machine** and **ironing machine** the schedule might be:

MONDAY: laundry work.
TUESDAY: mending.
WEDNESDAY: cleaning of silver, pantry and icebox with a legitimate afternoon out, whether it be housekeeper or maid.
THURSDAY: alternate a cleaning of living-room, hall and stairs with the cleaning of dining-room, hall and stairs.
FRIDAY: clean bedrooms and bath.
SATURDAY: kitchen and closet and icebox.

This same schedule without the **laundry equipment** must devote two days to the special work of the laundry rather than one and dovetail the mending with other work in consequence. In some houses laundry work is accomplished by outside service and for such a one we suggest the following:

> MONDAY: guest room, one other bedroom and bath; or alternate the remaining bedrooms and bath.
> TUESDAY: (alternate) do the living-room and dining-room.
> WEDNESDAY: clean silver, pantry and icebox.
> THURSDAY: clean the maid's room and do the fine hand ironing with an afternoon out.
> FRIDAY: Clean the kitchen, closets, and rear halls.
> SATURDAY: kitchen and closet and icebox.

WHEN ATTACHING A WINDOW SHADE

Instead of using hammer and tacks to attach a window shade to its roller, try the more satisfactory method of using inch-wide adhesive tape.

—Good Housekeeping Discovery.

A TABLE PAD

After I had had two extra leaves made for my dining-room table, I found that I could not match the leaves with table pads, so I took two strips of corrugated paper cut to fit the leaves, put them together having the corrugated sides inside, and tacked them together lightly in several places with heavy thread to keep them from slipping. This made a leaf the exact thickness of my other pads. I then made a slip-cover for them of flannelette, and found I had a satisfactory pad at slight cost.

—Good Housekeeping Discovery.

THE SINGLE MAID REGIME

AT BREAKFAST TIME

As there are six people in our household who come down to breakfast at different times in the morning, I found that instead of keeping the coffee hot over a low flame or reheating it each time, it is far better to pour the coffee from the percolator into a thermos bottle, which can be placed upon the table and used as it is needed. This method keeps the coffee hot, and the flavor is retained. —*Good Housekeeping Discovery.*

TIMING LONG DISTANCE TELEPHONE CALLS

We have occasion to use the telephone for many long-distance calls and have found the following method enables us to tell whether we have exceeded the allowed three minutes. A three-minute egg-timer is secured to the wall near the phone. When connection is made the egg-timer is turned and can be watched without taking your mind off the call. The timer is of the hour-glass type and the amount saved soon pays for its small cost.

—*Good Housekeeping Discovery.*

FOR HANGING BROOMS

I have found that small picture wire is far superior to any kind of twine for hanging brooms and brushes by, and the wire lasts indefinitely.

—*Good Housekeeping Discovery.*

CHAPTER II

The Routine with Two Servants

THE management of a home serviced by **two workers** is a bit more complicated. The housekeeper becomes a real employer of labor and has the added psychological problems to meet with which the man in business has to cope. The more executive ability, tact, and actual knowledge of the work itself, that she has at her command the more smoothly will the wheels of the machinery run. Many housekeepers do not realize that the acquisition of this additional pair of hands entails more real strain in house management. We exchange a work muscular in character and free from nerve strain for the mental effort of managing another's brain and hands. Many a housekeeper whose family is too large for the single worker looks back with longing to that period of less complicated living.

Perhaps the first step toward real management lies in their housing problem. But living conditions for service workers are almost universally good in these days. Separate beds, a bath, abundance of linen and warm bed clothing we

THE ROUTINE WITH TWO SERVANTS

all provide, but have we thought, in furnishing their rooms, to select furniture and rugs that will take a minimum of time and effort to keep them clean and spotless? This time and effort saved will redound to the credit side of your ledger. Simple beds, wicker furniture, cretonne cushions and curtains are all easy to clean and make for comfort and inexpensive beauty as well.

Again, efficiency is an overworked word but the housekeeper who knows her job inspires confidence in her workers that proves a magnet in itself. We have all noted with surprise the comparative ease with which the "driving" type of housekeeper has held her workers. Here is a partial explanation. That housekeeper may "drive" but because she knows what a given piece of work means in hours and effort she never expects the impossible. She can never be unfair and it is unfairness that labor can rightly resent. So if you will take the trouble to install a system that will extend from the budgeting of dollars to the budgeting of hours you will be more than repaid. I know of no printed lore that will completely suit your conditions. It is your washing which must be budgeted. It is your floors, rugs, meals and housecleaning that alone affect the issue and you must learn their requirements.

Even the working schedules that I am including are suggestive only. I doubt if they can be applied in a single case in their entirety. They should, however, have a suggestive value, inspiring you to try out your own plan.

BUSINESS OF HOUSEKEEPING

I hardly need to mention in these modern days the wisdom of providing proper tools for work as fast as there is any indication that they will be used. You cannot measure the value to you in connection with this service question of an attractive, well planned, convenient kitchen; of as attractive and well planned a laundry.

Engagement of Servants

In engaging servants take with you a **typewritten schedule** of the work required. Have it clearly understood that emergencies only would make it necessary to modify or change the schedule. After the servant is hired you can further help by giving all orders clearly and adhering to them after they are given, with the same emergency necessity provided for.

The question of time off should be fully settled in the preliminary interview. I cannot give you much help because local conditions make the amount and the time it is taken a variable factor, but I never had a worker who was not willing to effect some compromise between the conditions that my home demanded and her own wishes dictated. The point is not what hours and time you give but that those hours and time be definitely arranged for and once given be considered her very own.

Only the most serious emergencies should ever be permitted to interfere with the servant's outing. One who has never been in service cannot imagine the eagerness with which

THE ROUTINE WITH TWO SERVANTS

these breaks in their monotonous existence are looked forward to.

Order all supplies immediately after breakfast, using the list furnished by the cook or making up your own list. If dinner is in the middle of the day, Tuesday's supplies should be ordered on Monday. With the dinner pushed forward, store deliveries are so arranged that it is feasible to order on Monday morning for Monday's dinner needs. Written menus are a help, both in conserving supplies and in saving time of preparation.

THE TWO MAID RÉGIME

A common grouping of work under the **two maid system** calls for a **cook-laundress** and **chambermaid-waitress**. It is advisable to select both at the same time and preferably friends, not relatives, since friction is often more common in the latter case and far more difficult to deal with. If possible arrange for an interchange of work on the "days out." Make them see in a businesslike way that you are paying for service and it is obviously unfair to throw back upon you the burden of their work three afternoons out of the seven. It is often wise to be more liberal with the amount of time off, when they will agree to thus exchange their work. Another common arrangement is the couple: the man as houseman or butler; the woman as cook-laundress. In their selection personal references are even more essential than with any other type. Every house-

BUSINESS OF HOUSEKEEPING

keeper owes it to herself and her neighbor to require references from employees, and give them only when really earned. For much of the trouble from irresponsible service can be laid at the door of the housekeeper herself, in that she has allowed the standard of reference to be lowered —Let us regain that standard.

The following schedule of a week may have a suggestive value:

Cook-Laundress

MONDAY: demand a simple breakfast, omitting hot breads. Only such routine work as is necessary; and the washing. With the washing machine and an ironing machine it is not too much to expect the major part of the laundry work to be accomplished in one day. Meals for this day should be planned of the slow cooking variety requiring little time and effort on the part of the cook.

TUESDAY: routine work and hand ironing.

WEDNESDAY: routine work, clean icebox, kitchen floor and take the waitress's place in the afternoon.

THURSDAY: routine work, clean laundry, afternoon out.

FRIDAY: routine work, clean kitchen closets and cutlery.

Chambermaid-Waitress

MONDAY: routine work. Clean two bedrooms and bath. Alternate Mondays clean other bedrooms.

TUESDAY: routine work and clean silver, pantry.

WEDNESDAY: routine work, personal washing. Afternoon out.

THURSDAY: clean living-room, or dining-room on alternate Thursdays. Serve the dinner. Some simple cooking may be involved.

FRIDAY: alternate cleaning guest rooms or the servants' rooms and all bedroom closets.

THE ROUTINE WITH TWO SERVANTS

Cook-Laundress
SATURDAY: routine work, clean icebox and halls, and kitchen floors.
SUNDAY: only most necessary work and alternate Sunday out, either immediately after an early dinner or for the balance of day according to agreement.

Chambermaid-Waitress
SATURDAY: routine work, halls and stairs.
SUNDAY: only most necessary work and alternate Sunday out, either immediately after an early dinner or for the balance of day according to agreement.

AN EXCELLENT WAY TO UTILIZE SCRAPS OF TOILET SOAP

Save all odds and ends of toilet soap of every description. When enough has accumulated, grate in very small pieces and put through the food-chopper, using the medium cutter first, and then the fine cutter. To one cupful of this granulated soap add one and one-half cupfuls of corn-meal and put through the food-chopper again until reduced to a coarse meal. This may be facilitated by rubbing between the hands to loosen the particles. When all will pass readily through a meal sieve, add one ounce of olive oil to each two and one-half cupfuls of the soap and cornmeal mixture. Blend thoroughly. An ordinary fruit jar with the rubber ring in place makes a good container. A quantity of this soap powder kept on the kitchen sink or in the bathroom will be found invaluable for cleansing very soiled hands and keeping them soft and smooth, besides being perfectly harmless and costing next to nothing.

—*Good Housekeeping Discovery.*

SECTION III

Routine Household Tasks

Chapter. I—The Daily Routine of Downstairs Care
Chapter II—The Daily Routine of Upstairs Care
Chapter III—Dishwashing Three Times a Day
Chapter IV—The Care of the Refrigerator

CHAPTER I

The Daily Routine of Downstairs Care

BECAUSE these directions for care of downstairs rooms are so concrete and explicit they may not conform in all details with your requirements; but they can be so easily revised to meet a varying need in the individual family as to time and special duties, that I offer them as a guide to any housekeeper who wishes to plan a routine of work either for herself or a paid helper.

Be on duty and ready for work downstairs at 7:30 A. M. Open **front hall door and dining- and living-room windows** for a few moments to give them a thorough airing. This is even more necessary in winter than in summer months when the house is presumably open during the night as well as the day.

While the windows are open "tidy" the **hall and living-room.** Replace magazines, and fold newspapers, but do not destroy them until next day. Restore misplaced furniture, adjust slip covers trimly, and "plump" all cushions.

BUSINESS OF HOUSEKEEPING

Empty ash trays and nut bowls. Remove any wilted flowers. This is especially important. No room looks fresh and inviting with flowers other than of the freshest. Give the same attention to the living-room porch, the library or den, or both of them. The before breakfast care is much more of a freshening process than a "cleaning," as you will see. Indeed in most families the "clutter" is often confined to the one favorite room, be it den, living-porch or library, so that while all of them have to be planned for in the schedule, the half-hour allowed is ample to thus care for all the rooms.

Next set the **breakfast table.** Sort the mail, and place the letters on the table at their respective cover places. Serve breakfast at 8 o'clock. Keep the coffee hot for late comers by covering the percolator as it stands on the table with a tea cozy. Do not try to keep it hot in the kitchen. An electric grill in the butler's pantry is excellent for this if used on "low" heat.

Immediately after breakfast clear the table and wash the silver only. Then complete the routine care of the living-room before washing dishes. If possible sandwich some of this work between serving breakfast to the late ones, if there should be any.

Dust mop the **living-porch floor.** Water the window box plants. Wash and fill the dog's water trays. Empty and wash ash trays. Then dust, using one of the dustless cloths rather than furniture polish, because this furniture is

THE DAILY ROUTINE OF DOWNSTAIRS CARE

painted. For stained willow the polish cloth may be used. In the **living-room,** see that the wood basket has a supply of medium sized wood, and kindling if necessary. Keep a small fire laid unless the hearth is so hot that the wood might ignite. Sweep the **hearth** with a small hearth brush. Empty waste paper baskets, ash trays and smoking stands. Throw away no newspapers or magazines that are not in waste baskets. Dust mop the **floor** and run the carpet sweeper over the rug. Dust, if necessary. This last direction may need a word of explanation. Because of the presence of two dogs in my own household, one a long-haired Pekingese with a wonderful coat, the other an Irish Terrier, rug care was absolutely essential in this house every morning, but because a vacuum cleaner is used for the weekly rug cleaning, daily dusting is rarely necessary, especially in summer, although the house is within two hundred feet of a main traveled road. But let your own requirements govern this direction.

Fill the **flower vases** if in summer and polish the **silver vases, candlesticks,** etc., with a quick wipe, using a silver polishing cloth instead of a duster. In tidying the rooms keep one place, a convenient drawer or a large tray basket in a wood standard, for the small personal belongings that might have been left out of place by any member of the family. It saves time on the part of the worker as well as the careless one who otherwise must hunt for a small, but needed possession. Put everything, of whose

BUSINESS OF HOUSEKEEPING

proper place you are in the least doubtful, in this basket. As soon as you have finished with the living-room you may wash dishes. Next run the **carpet sweeper** over the dining-room rug and dust the room carefully. Pay special attention to **window sills** and trim in summer and the **radiator** or **register** in winter, when each is the main source of dust. In dusting this room, again don't forget to use the silver polishing cloth for a quick wipe-over of any silver pieces that may be on table, buffet or serving table. Rub the **furniture,** especially the table top, with the merest suspicion, a drop or two, of either furniture polish or liquid wax, on a silk or velvetine cloth. Polish with a clean dry cloth. Should you find a white fog mark, it can be removed by wiping over with a cloth wrung as dry as possible from hot water, to which a few drops of ammonia have been added. Finish by **polishing** with furniture polish. Heat marks are not so easily removed, but a daily rub of this character will act as a preventive for many scars and will make those already there much better in appearance.

Occasionally a **grease spot** is found on a seat cushion. If of hair-cloth, scrub with soap and only enough water to moisten the brush. If of leather, you must use more oil, preferably neat's foot, rubbing the entire surface to give it a uniform color. By the way, **leather furniture** should be given this oil rub occasionally, preferably at the time of the spring or fall house cleaning, in order to prevent the leather from drying and cracking.

THE DAILY ROUTINE OF DOWNSTAIRS CARE

Some one may suggest that this routine of daily care is suitable only where maid service is available. On the contrary, if the housekeeper herself must attend to it the schedule offers the best of preparation for her day of specialized toil. For not one of us but works more easily in kitchen or laundry for the assurance of a tidy house.

Again, it is an ideal responsibility for the small son and daughter, since not one of the tasks involved is beyond their strength and it is a type of work that will help to overcome their own tendency to leave their possessions where they last used them.

ANOTHER USE FOR THE BLOTTER

When you upset the bowl of flowers on the waxed or varnished surface of your mahogany table, instead of using a cloth or towel, rush to your desk and get a blotter. The absorbent surface will soak up the water, leaving neither smear nor cloudy mark.

—*Good Housekeeping Discovery.*

WHEN GREASE DROPS ON THE FLOOR

If grease is spilled on the floor throw ice-cold water on it immediately, or the coldest water available. This will harden the grease so that it will not soak into the wood of the floor to any great extent, and it will be a comparatively easy matter to clean the floor.

—*Good Housekeeping Discovery.*

BUSINESS OF HOUSEKEEPING

INDISPENSABLE TO THE KITCHEN

I have found a thick cardboard about twenty-four by eighteen inches in size covered tightly with oilcloth almost indispensable in the kitchen. I use it to protect my table or oven top from the blackened bottoms of pans or greasy or wet dishes or kitchen ware. It can be easily and quickly wiped off, and takes the place of newspapers which many people use but are rather unsightly after being used once.
—*Good Housekeeping Discovery.*

INK SPOTS ON THE FLOOR

When ink is spilled on any waxed floor, hardwood or soft wood, mop it up quickly with a soft cloth. Then rub the spot with fine steel wool wet in clear warm water. Finish with a clean wet cloth, allow to dry, and apply wax. Not a trace of ink will be left if you work quickly.
—*Good Housekeeping Discovery.*

RAISING THE KITCHEN TABLE

A kitchen table that is too low for a tall woman to work at comfortably may serve a double purpose. Cover it with white table oilcloth (or zinc or glass if the pocketbook permits) and have a carpenter or the "handy man about the house" make a second table top raised on four supports to the proper height. The original surface then makes a convenient shelf for many small utensils and kitchen accessories.   —*Good Housekeeping Discovery.*

THE DAILY ROUTINE OF DOWNSTAIRS CARE

FOR SCRATCHED FURNITURE

When we moved recently, several pieces of walnut furniture were badly scratched—not great gouges, such as would make refinishing absolutely necessary; just unsightly scratches. Mother cut about one-quarter of an inch from one end of a brazil nut kernel, rubbed this freshly-cut oily surface over the scratches, and they disappeared. Of course, the depressions are still there, but the ugly whitish streaks are obliterated. Now, whoever does the dusting in our house does it with a piece of brazil nut kernel in her work-apron pocket. —*Good Housekeeping Discovery.*

MORE KITCHEN TABLE SPACE

If you need more table or shelf room in your kitchen, make an oilcloth slip for your ironing-board table, stand it in a convenient place, and you will find it a real help. The oilcloth slip may be easily removed on ironing day, and you make your ironing board do double service.

—*Good Housekeeping Discovery.*

CHAPTER II

The Daily Routine of Upstairs Care

So soon as the downstairs general work is completed, go upstairs to the rooms already left airing by their occupants .

Tidy the **bathrooms** first. Clean and disinfect the **bowls**, wipe off **faucets**. Wash and replace **drinking glasses**. Wash **floor** only once a week unless needed. Return any supplies to **medicine cabinet**. Wash the tub, even though each user accomplishes the same task. Renew **soap**, and bathroom supplies from the store shelf. Keep in the bathroom a basket containing a package of friction powder especially adapted for use on porcelain, and enamel; a flannel polishing cloth for the nickel, long handled woven wire brushes for use in the bowl and bath tub, a bottle of any household disinfectant and finally a bottle of a mixture of half turpentine and half water with enough oil of lavender to cut the odor. There is nothing better for cleaning porcelain and enamel than a small quantity of this mixture applied on the brush and followed by a

THE DAILY ROUTINE OF UPSTAIRS CARE

scrubbing with hot water. Even the sticky deposit from hard water yields.

Renew **linen** from the linen closet. Hang fresh linen towels of two sizes as well as bath towels. Be sure to give the guest bath room an inspection visit, even though there be no guest.

"Do up" one room at a time. **P**ut away garments and shoes. Disturb personal possessions as little as possible. Tidy around them. The very first step in **bed making** is bed airing. Be sure that both big and little members of a family open windows wide and throw clothes and pad clear back over the footboard in order that air and sun may reach them. It is not necessary to turn a mattress every day; once a week is ample to keep any mattress in good condition.

At the same time put on fresh linen, changing both lower and upper sheets. Some housekeepers prefer to use the upper sheet again as a lower and thus reduce the linen laundry. There can be no real objection, so let the individual preference govern this. The point is to have a system and use it, making the change each week on the same day. In my home, Saturday is the day. Pillowcases are changed twice each week, oftener if there happens to be a victim of insomnia to consider. A fresh pillowcase is a real invitation to slumber.

Much more comfort is afforded where the slip is selected large enough in size that the pillow may have freedom.

BUSINESS OF HOUSEKEEPING

A tight pillow-case means a hard, tight bundle under the shoulders and head. It wears the pillow-case, it wears the pillow, and it wears the nerves of the sleeper. Learn to use pillows as flat as possible.

Next, use a **soft floor mop,** paying especial attention to the floor under beds. The downy fluff found there is not dust but the fluff from blankets. Better still, run the vacuum cleaner over the bare floor, once a week. Also once a week use the wax or oil polish mop, and vacuum clean the rugs. Dust a sleeping room every day. Wipe off dressing-tables and dressers if glass covered. Dust if linen covered, and renew linen only when needed. Once a month is ample where daily care is thus given.

Remove thermos water jugs and carry downstairs to be filled for use the following night. See that all candlesticks have candles in them with a safety match box at hand for lighting in emergency.

Finally, dustmop the hall, and on laundry day sort and put away the clean linen. Carry the basket filled with ''mending'' into the sewing room for attention there.

Beds and Bed-Making

Just a word about the choice of equipment. There is real reasoning as well as fashion in the growing use of **single beds.** Children are more comfortable, less likely to transmit the annoying, small infections of childhood, and finally, far less apt to develop a tendency to restlessness

THE DAILY ROUTINE OF UPSTAIRS CARE

and the insomnia of later life. It is a child's right to sleep alone from the standpoint of his health even more than his comfort.

But a practical difficulty immediately arises. Many a home is already equipped with double beds and cannot see its way clear to scrap expensive equipment. One mother solved this by cutting her wide sheets in two and making each half of the bed separately. She even alternated head and foot for the two little occupants. Again, when room space is an item, use the narrow two-feet six-inch boarding-school bed. It can be found in simple metal designs.

Single beds for comfortable sleeping do not necessarily have to be expensive beds. A choice of wood or metal can now be made without loss of tight, sanitary construction in the case of wooden beds, or loss of beauty in the case of metal beds. Indeed these latter are now made simulating the wood beds in line, color, and finish.

The simplest of **springs** can be chosen with little difference in comfort on these narrow beds, but box springs have an advantage when the first cost can be afforded, in the lessened care required to keep them clean and free from dust.

If you have suffered discomfort in one of the expensive box-spring-equipped beds, here may be a solution. Insert two half- or three-quarter-inch blocks of wood on both sides beneath the spring at both the head and at the center of the bed. This will make the spring more

BUSINESS OF HOUSEKEEPING

nearly level and therefore comfortable. In making box-springs a manufacturer has stated it is not possible to tuft them as much at head and foot and therefore, until the bed has been slept in long enough to take up this difference there is an unpleasant drop at the head.

In selecting the **mattress**, however, be careful to choose a softer one than would be permissible on a wide bed. It may be of any chosen filling so long as this specification is filled. If of hair, be sure it is not packed firmly and closely. I realize this is radical advice; but I have tried both kinds and found that every person who slept on a certain narrow bed equipped with a most expensive, firmly packed hair mattress was an eager candidate for a change in room quarters. It was not the bed or the spring, for comfort came on the identical bed equipped with a softer mattress. By the way, these are long-lived on single beds, for they do not sag or get out of shape.

I wonder if we realize the strides that have been made in **pillow** construction. In the old home are still the "down" pillows with which my grandmother as a bride equipped her home. "Down," did I say? Yes, it was as near down as the crude hand-picking methods could obtain, but these pillows weigh heavy indeed beside the present day manufacture of similar rated quality. In selecting, make sure that your pillows are made of cleanly, new materials and in a cleanly way. Buy only those marked with a tag stating this fact. Pillow contents can carry infection, so it is well worth while to guard against this possibility.

THE DAILY ROUTINE OF UPSTAIRS CARE

Just a word about length in **sheets and blankets**. Extra length means far more comfort and correspondingly less work in keeping bedding clean. The stock sizes 99-inch or 108-inch length sheets are the only two permissible. The narrow 63-inch sheet is often difficult to find in the longer dimension, so I give the 99-inch alternative, but buy the longer one when you can, for it affords ample material both for tucking in deeply at the foot and for a protecting covering for the blankets. Incidentally I have never seen either length procurable in a "special sale."

Blankets can easily be lengthened with a 14-inch strip of strong cotton flannel stitched across the bottom. All this can be used for tucking at the foot, leaving the high-priced wool as the real bed covering. It is not always easy to purchase long blankets in the retail shops, although the manufacturers make them a full 90 inches. I am taking it for granted that you cut your blankets in two and bind both halves.

The **top covering** for a bed may, of course, be as elaborate and beautiful as one pleases, but the simple dimity or light-weight washable spread is excellent for every-day family use. The beds look well; they can easily be kept looking well; and the process of undressing the bed for occupancy is not so tedious and annoying that the family rebel and a single overworked maid must be asked to make the rounds for this preparation.

BUSINESS OF HOUSEKEEPING

As a final suggestion for equipment, see that every **mattress** has its **quilted pad,** both for protection and comfort. This pad smooths out the tuftings of the mattress and prevents an occasional hair from penetrating both mattress cover and sheet to the discomfort of the sleeper.

When ready for the actual making of the bed, spread the **mattress pad** smoothly over the mattress. Next open the sheet and turn under at the foot on both sides, using the same amount of sheet to insure a straight line at the foot. Do not try to make one whole side of a bed before you go around to the other side, even at the cost of more steps, because the taut, smooth unwrinkled lower sheet so necessary to comfort cannot be secured unless an even tucking in at the foot is first secured. Now pull the sheet smooth and as tight as you can at either top side. This smooth sleeping surface is the secret of comfort.

In the same way put on the **top sheet,** though in this case it is seldom necessary to work on both sides of the bed for smoothing out of the top section, since the arms will reach over any but the wider beds. The only thing to be careful of is that the line at the foot is a straight line. Use enough sheet for tucking in to secure strength. If a bed is thus started, it can be remade next day with very little attention to the foot, since even the most restless of sleepers cannot pull the clothes out of line.

There is a bit of a wrinkle in putting on a blanket that needs a word of explanation. *F*irst, if your blankets are short, lay one of them on the bed, reaching only to the foot and with no attempt to tuck it in.

Lay the second one lower down to give you plenty of "tuck-in" material, and you will find that it will hold the first one securely in place, giving strength and shoulder warmth as well. When the blanket is tucked squarely under the mattress at the foot, lay each side back and over the mattress along the side until the side edge of the blanket is at right angles with the bottom line of the mattress. Now tuck the lower edge of blanket smoothly under the mattress, then bring the whole blanket down over mattress side and fold smoothly under it. You will find that you have a clean-cut diagonal fold line, and that it holds the clothes as if in a vise against the most active childish or adult restlessness. Don't try to follow this direction mentally. Perform each stage of the task as directed and the puzzling directions clarify much as knitting or crocheting directions do.

WHEN SCRUBBING THE TUB

The brushes sold by various manufacturers to be used for cleaning the toilet bowl are just right for the bath tub as well, and save a great deal of stooping and kneeling and reaching when the tub is scrubbed.

—Good Housekeeping Discovery.

A NEW USE FOR ADHESIVE TAPE

If adhesive tape is put on the sharp angle at the foot of a bed-spring frame, accidental three-cornered tears in one's sheets will be eliminated. Where the youngsters make their own beds, I found that the above idea helped considerably. —*Good Housekeeping Discovery.*

TO KEEP THE DRESSER MIRROR IN PLACE

When the mirror on a dresser is fastened on in such a way that it will not stay at a desirable angle, either through wear or otherwise, there is one sure way of making it stay, and that is to place between the mirror frame and the post a cube of Art Gum. They can be had at the ten-cent store at two for a nickel, and beat paper wads and other materials, because they will stick in place, can be easily moved, and are out of sight. Try it and be surprised! —*Good Housekeeping Discovery.*

TO CLEAN COMBS

The quickest and most completely successful way to clean a comb is to use the ordinary string comb cleaner slightly moistened with carbon tetrachloride. The grease solvent instantly dissolves the oil which holds the soil on the comb. leaving it as clean as when new. Any of the commercial spot removers or dry cleaning preparations may be used instead of carbon tetrachloride, though the latter, being non-proprietary, is sometimes cheaper.

—*Good Housekeeping Discovery.*

AN EFFICIENT BATHROOM

I find that my bathroom is kept in better order when I provide a towel bar for each member of the family, with

THE DAILY ROUTINE OF UPSTAIRS CARE

two rust-proof hooks at the side of each bar. One hook is for the tooth brush, and one for the wash cloth, which always has a tape sewed in one corner for hanging it up. On another wall, I keep one or two towel bars for guests, and in an inconspicuous corner I have a hook for my cleaning cloth which is hemmed with a loop for hanging. Beside the cleaning cloth is a nail for the scrubbing brush, and in the medicine closet is a shelf reserved for cleaning powder and soap. I step into the bathroom on my morning cleaning round, and find all my materials at hand, with no need to waste steps collecting them.

—*Good Housekeeping Discovery.*

A NEW USE FOR A RUBBER SPONGE

Quite accidentally I discovered that an old rubber sponge is excellent for cleaning the porcelain in the bathroom. It retains the scouring powder, produces a good amount of friction, and does not become stringy as a cloth does. It is easily rinsed, and is a joy to handle.

—*Good Housekeeping Discovery.*

FOR THE SURFACE OF THE DRESSING-TABLE

The surface of the child's or young girl's dressing-table is only too often marred by nicks or spilled perfume, lotions, etc. Glass tops are expensive, but a thick blotter cut to the exact size needed is a splendid substitute. It does not show under the cover, and prolongs the life of furniture.

—*Good Housekeeping Discovery.*

CHAPTER III

Dishwashing Three Times a Day

ASSEMBLE your tools first of all. If you have a machine for **washing dishes** see that it is clean and ready. For hand washing you will need a dish pan, preferably of the fiber variety, a capacious dish drainer, a soap shaker, a dish mop or dishwashing brush, and plenty of clean, dry towels and scrubbing cloths.

For the **silver and china** use only a neutral soap or soap preparation. It is a safe rule to purchase only this type of soap for kitchen use. Surely the dishes one eats from are as important to have washed with a neutral soap as one's hands.

For the **cooking dishes** provide friction powders, soap powders and steel wool.

You will need a **sink drainer** to scrape the remnants into and you will need refrigerator dishes, preferably enamel, to hold the leftovers.

DISHWASHING THREE TIMES A DAY

Clear the dining-table and care for leftover food first of all. Never put it away in serving dishes. If you clear the table by courses, dispose of the food from each course as you bring it into the kitchen. Do not place in the refrigerator, however, until it has cooled.

Complete the dining-room work, folding cloth and silence cloth or luncheon set, and sending the napkins to laundry when necessary. Never put linen back into the drawer if it is not to be again used.

Return to kitchen, scrape all dishes clean into the sink drainer, pile in as compact a space as possible on a table or the drainboard farthest away from the china closet. Wash and dry toward their final destination.

Sort the **cooking dishes** and fill with water. If there should be any with burned on food add a teaspoon or more of washing soda, and allow to heat while you are washing the china. The most stubborn kettle will yield to this treatment. For aluminum kettles, this method is not suitable—instead use steel wool; if badly burned allow to heat, dry, directly over the fire; when the burned portion will chip off; finish with the steel wool.

Next rinse off silver and china, using either warm or cold water. One of the **faucet attachments** for washing dishes is ideal for this purpose. Even without one, however, you can hold each dish under the faucet until flushed off with the aid of dish mop or brush. The stream of water may be a very tiny one and still do the work quickly. Be

BUSINESS OF HOUSEKEEPING

especially careful with dinner plates, salad plates, dessert and serving dishes. **Glassware,** unless used for serving dishes, does not need this rinse.

They are now ready either for packing into the machine or for a hot soapy wash. Use water far too hot for the hand to bear and a suds made with the soap shaker filled with soap. Put the silver in first and lift out as soon as clean with the aid of the dish mop, placing in the dish drainer.

Next wash the glasses, one at a time. Dry immediately without further rinsing and while both silver and glasses are almost too hot to touch. They will dry with a glisten that will astonish you.

Next wash cups, saucers, bread and butter plates, etc. The plates and saucers may be placed in a pile in the hot soapy water, washed and removed one at a time. But the cups should be handled singly.

Never have a mass of dishes in your dishpan.

Renew water and soap as often as it cools so that it no longer heats the dishes. For that is the secret of this method. Have the water so hot that the dishes dry with a polish and have the water so clean that they will not need another riuse. I have used this method in summer where the tea kettle was the only source of hot water, and I found that instead of using more, I needed less hot water, and fewer dish towels. Remember the dishes are

DISHWASHING THREE TIMES A DAY

practically clean before you start to wash them, and they are practically dry from heat before you start to dry them.

Dry cups and small plates with the china towels. Renew water and wash dinner, salad and dessert plates, next and in their order.

Wipe each set as soon as washed, placing the next in the hot water while you are drying the first. Put away in china closet unless you have a service wagon that can be loaded for but one or two trips.

Renew hot water and wash each serving dish and platter with the suds. Wipe silver platters dry promptly and while still very hot. The tarnish which is due to the action of moisture left on these platters is reddish in color and the hardest of all types to remove even with silver cleaners. They must be wiped perfectly dry after each use. This prevention is the best of all cures.

Next wash **mixing bowls, cooking bowls and baking dishes** of the vitrified china, pottery or glass variety. If these have been soaking in water they will not be hard to do. The brown caramel stains of the cooking dishes can be quickly removed with a mat of steel wool.

Stack these dishes neatly in the drainer and rinse with a pitcher of hot water. Notice that this is the first time you have needed this rinse. Dry only after thorough draining.

Next wash **saucepans and roasting pan or broiler.** And now is the time to tackle the saucepan that has been heat-

BUSINESS OF HOUSEKEEPING

ing with washing soda. When each one is clean wipe as **dry** as possible with your dish cloth wrung dry, then place on the stove to become thoroughly dry. Place them on the back of a coal range or on top of the gas oven with **one** burner turned very low.

Lastly, **wash coffee or tea pot** directly under a faucet of fresh water if possible. Empty grounds first, then use plenty of water, a clean brush with scouring soap and steel wool, but no soap suds. When clean wipe and place on range to complete drying. Rinse out the dish pan and fill again with hot soapy water. Let the dish towels stand in this while the kitchen is tidied and the food put away. Then wash them, rinse quickly and hang them in the air to dry. Finish the task of dish washing by washing the sink out with hot suds and a mop. I only accent the mop because the water should be too hot for the hand. For routine use nothing else is needed for a white sink of any variety. The red stains due to iron will yield to a very weak acid solution. And the brownish stains due to other salts in the water supply are best removed by an occasional application of Javelle Water but no gritty powder should ever be used. Once the fine sheen is marred constant scouring is needed. Try the hot suds treatment and I am sure you will be convinced.

It is more than possible that some housekeepers who have used other methods of washing dishes, stacking them in a drainer and allowing them to dry after a hot rinse may

DISHWASHING THREE TIMES A DAY

think the method outlined entails more work, but where the number of dishes amount to more than a single drainer load you may find it a quicker method. But even in a small family it is a practical method of teaching and always results in the spotless china we demand for our tables.

ELIMINATING THE DISHPAN

I keep a servantless house in these days of high-priced help, and hence try to reduce the housework to a minimum amount of energy expended. In place of using the ordinary hot dishpan to clean my dishes, I have attached to the hot water faucet of the kitchen a bath-tub spray, the nozzle end of which is equipped with the usual rubber brush through which the water passes. I arrange my dishes in a large wire drain basket, which I place in the sink. I then turn the warm water on full force and direct the powerful spray upon the dishes. The water striking them with such force readily cleans the sides of the dishes which it strikes. I then turn off the water and rearrange my dishes so that when I turn on the warm spray again, it will strike the reverse side. Then I rinse them with hot water. Cooking utensils I clean separately with the spray. Where food has adhered solidly to them, the mere spray alone will not thoroughly clean them. In such cases I rub the rubber brush nozzle, with the warm water turned on full force, against them. The combined force of the water and rubbing action of the brush thoroughly cleans them.

—*Good Housekeeping Discovery.*

TO DRY A DISH MOP

Stand your dish mop in an empty milk bottle to dry. The stick will be stationary, and the disheveled top-knot will sun nicely before a kitchen window and keep sweet and clean. —*Good Housekeeping Discovery.*

DOCTORING DISH TOWELS

When your dish towels become so thin and "slimpsey" that they get soaked through almost immediately, try stitching two of them together, and you will find they have double life and you double comfort in using them. They need not be the same size. Set the smaller one neat and straight on the other and stitch along the edge. I also use up worn bedroom towels in this way. They are often of nice huck or damask, but too shabby for the bedroom; put two together, and you have a splendidly absorbent dish towel. I do not recommend this process for hand towels, as the double thickness will annoy in such use, but for dish towels I find it a great success.

—*Good Housekeeping Discovery.*

CHAPTER IV

The Care of the Refrigerator

I DO not know of any department of housework that has been more influenced by new methods of manufacture than the care of the **refrigerator**. The daily or weekly scalding scrub used to be absolutely necessary because a mold or bacteria might easily lurk in the seams of the lining if any less drastic method were used. Destruction of all germs and molds are far more important than any possible consideration of ice economy.

Today, however, this is not true; the manufacturer supplies sanitary seamless linings and the wise housekeeper takes advantage of this fact by revising her routine care. Such a refrigerator should receive daily attention if any food is spilled. Shelves may be removed, cleaned and cooled before returning. But into the refrigerator itself should go only a cloth wrung out of cold water to which a generous amount of baking soda has been added. Work quickly and as soon as the damage is repaired wipe dry with a clean cloth. This method saves not only the ice con-

BUSINESS OF HOUSEKEEPING

sumption but food spoilage as well, because if warm or hot water is used, the box is filled with condensing moisture and food tends to spoil more quickly in such atmospheres.

The new refrigerator, then, is kept clean by care in its use. Never use scalding water in the food compartment. Even in the drain, use it only when absolutely necessary, substituting **a weekly brushing** with strong sal soda water. Any odorless disinfectant may be used here as well, but be sure that it *is* odorless.

There are times when the drastic **scalding** treatment is indicated—as after any serious food spoilage, or if the ice has been entirely melted before replenishment was possible. Under such conditions use plenty of scalding soda water, then wipe dry and air thoroughly before closing the box. Just before closing wipe again with a dry absorbent linen towel to trap any possible moisture.

Finally, just a few words about placement and seasonal care. Never keep a refrigerator on a porch or exposed to the elements in any way. Remember it is a delicate bit of cabinet work and will deteriorate so fast as to seriously affect your investment. If space forces it onto the porch, build a substantial closet for it with a waterproof roof and double hung doors, opening down the center to the full width of the refrigerator. Such a housing protects your refrigerator and conserves its ice consumption.

THE CARE OF THE REFRIGERATOR

At least once a year renew the finish—varnish, shellac, or enamel painted, depending on its original coat. In this way you will prevent any possible warping of the wood in case of "sweating."

And this sweating, by the way, may result from any one or both of two conditions. The first one is unavoidable. It is not humanly possible to so insulate the box that there will be no apparent difference between the temperatures of the outside casing of the box and the room. Because the room temperature is higher any humidity in the air of the room is bound to show as condensation on the outside of the box. It is, of course, worse on moisture laden "dog days." The only way to prevent it in time warping the doors by seeping into the wood, is to keep the moisture wiped off and give the box a weekly rub with any wax or oil furniture polish. This fills the wood pores and repels the moisture. The second condition is even more within your control. The iceman in chipping a cake of ice to fit your needs often leaves tiny bits of ice or a small amount of water on the ice compartment ledge. In time the door does not fit "quite so well" and trouble starts through warping. Watch this ledge then and keep it **dry**.

SECTION IV

Special Household Tasks

Chapter   I—Silver Cleaning
Chapter   II—Metal Cleaning
Chapter   III—Floor Treatment and Care
Chapter   IV—Furniture Cleaning and Polishing
Chapter   V—Closet and Storeroom Care
Chapter   VI—Cellar Care and Cleanliness
Chapter VII—Spring Renovating
Chapter VIII—Seasonal Housecleaning
Chapter   IX—Safe Procedure in Closing a House

CHAPTER I

The Task of Cleaning Silver

SELECT one day in the week's routine for **silver cleaning.** Wednesday afternoon, immediately after luncheon, works well in my household, since laundry is disposed of and Thursday is the usual short day.

Provide yourself with the proper **supplies and tools.** You will need silver-cleaning compounds in powder, paste or liquid form; a small brush and flannel cloths for application of the compound. Provide two silver polishing cloths, one for upstairs use and one for downstairs use as dusting polishers. It is a question whether to include one of the electrolytic cleaning-plates, to be used in an enameled kettle of water containing its proper proportion of salt and soda. The sole disadvantage of the outfit is the tendency there seems to be to offer by house-to-house canvass thin strips of metal too small to be of any practical value. The charge is often exorbitant with as exorbitant claims for efficiency. Oftentimes there is a false claim made of Good Housekeeping Institute approval. Therefore, be sure that the plate you purchase is generous in size and reasonably thick, with no sharp edges, and that the price is reasonable. And by the way an aluminum pie tin used upside down in the kettle makes an excellent easily cleaned plate for this purpose.

Mentally divide the **house silver** into two groups: the table silver, flat ware, serving dishes and platters should be cleaned as one operation. Dressing-table fittings, vases, candlesticks, and silver ornaments are a separate task better accomplished on a separate day. Unless you are near the seashore or in otherwise trying climate conditions this latter group may not need a drastic cleaning for months, especially if you use one of the new silver lacquers that protect the metal from oxidation.

Daily care consists merely of dusting them with a **silver polishing cloth** instead of the usual buffer in the process of daily tidying. Thus, in one pocket of your apron tuck a duster; in the other pocket keep a silver polishing cloth. Dust the china vase with a regular duster but use the polishing cloth for the silver vase. Such daily care takes no added time and is invaluable in saving real work with the larger pieces. If silver ware is imperfectly dried after washing it is far more difficult to keep clean and get clean because of a chemical action of the water. You can save yourself much work then by thoroughly drying all table ware either flat or serving dishes before putting it away.

THE TASK OF CLEANING SILVER

When ready for the task assemble all the silver that must be cleaned and brush and dust out carefully the silver drawer compartment.

Cleaning by Electrolysis

If you use the **electrolytic** method, here is the proper procedure. Into an enamel kettle of boiling hot water place a teaspoonful each of salt and baking soda to each quart of water used. Place a strip of aluminum in the bottom of the kettle, next add the flat silver helter-skelter and leave in for five minutes. Keep the water at boiling temperature. Each piece should touch another piece to make a continuous connection with the aluminum when the silver will all be cleaned perfectly of its tarnish, even though every piece does not actually touch the plate. Because the process involves a chemical reaction the silver must be removed to a pan filled with warm water soap suds and washed thoroughly to remove any soil that may have been softened by the process. Then rinse and dry. If you do not like the hard brightness of this clean silver; use, as I do, one of the silver polishing cloths for a final rub. The result is a beautifully soft polish.

The method is especially excellent for **flat** silver because it is so ideally clean. It is a safe method to use on all plain or brushed silver, either solid or plated. It should never be used on any metal of whose composition you have any doubt. Oxidized finish from silver and silver plate is immediately destroyed in this cleaning process, so never use it when you want to retain this grayed finish. German silver and metal alloys commonly used in bag tops, etc., are ruined because they are not really silver or silver plate. So-called Dutch silver is not pure silver and should be cleaned only with soap, water and polishing cloth. Even the solid silver and plated silver in so-called Dutch design should be cleaned by this process only when its attractive oxidizing is no longer desired.

But even though you adopt the electrolytic method of cleaning silver there still must remain a miscellaneous group that had better be cleaned with a paste or powder or a cleaning compound applied on a cloth. A tooth brush makes an excellent tool to clean heavily chased pieces. Apply the cleaning compound, rub until clean, brush out the accumulated compound from all crevices, wash in hot soap suds, dry, and polish with a silver polishing cloth.

Always finish your tasks by replacing the silver in its respective places, and scour the aluminum plate so that it will be bright and shining ready for its next use. Many housekeepers do not realize that the efficiency of the plate depends upon its being scoured clean down to the bright metal after each use.

Keep the polishing cloth protected in a box of tin or wood and wash only often enough to insure cleanliness. Rinse out the flannel cloths and brushes and pack away the entire cleaning outfit in a small box or a basket devoted to its purpose.

BLOTTERS FOR THE EMERGENCY

I keep a pack of large, plain, white blotters in the drawer of my sideboard, and when anything is spilled on the dining-room linen, instead of reaching for a freshly laundered napkin to sop it up with, I reach at once for one of the blotters, and the spilled liquid is absorbed immediately instead of being made larger by useless sopping. This simple process saves considerable time in laundering, because if it happens that milk or water has been overturned, the blotter takes up the moisture so quickly and thoroughly that the accident may often pass entirely unnoticed, and the linen may be used several times more. On the other hand, if the stain is of fruit or coffee, the blotter system is equally efficient in that what there is of the spot is much smaller in area, so that there is less linen to be rubbed and scalded.   —*Good Housekeeping Discovery.*

CARE IN USING ELECTRICITY

Now that electrical devices of all kinds are so constantly used, many women forget that certain precautions must be taken in their use. Never turn electricity on or off when you are standing on a wet or even damp floor. If you do so, the current is apt to pass through your body. This advice is particularly applicable to the kitchen, bathroom, and laundry where water is most likely to be spilled.

—*Good Housekeeping Discovery.*

CHAPTER II

Metal Cleaning

BRASS, copper and nickel have been metals used so liberally in house fittings that they have proved real items in the work of the careful housekeeper. Even today there is some of this to cope with, but not in anything like the quantity which the olden time housekeeper was possessed of.

Brass and copper should first be cleaned with a **metal polish**. It is not enough to apply the compound and dry and polish the metal. Both metals will stay clean longer if after polishing they are washed in hot water to remove every bit of polish. Wipe dry and give them a final rub with a paste made of rottenstone with enough raw linseed oil to make into a paste. After these metals are once cleaned, however, they can be covered with a **lacquer** which will protect them from oxidizing changes and resulting tarnish for a considerable period.

But if you intend to use the lacquer omit the final rub with rottenstone and oil. Instead, wipe the metal over with denatured alcohol so that every bit of moisture will

METAL CLEANING

be removed. Apply the lacquer with a soft brush. Two coats of lacquer are preferable, to be sure that no "bald spots" are left on the metal. Allow about a half-hour between the coats. On door knockers, locks, and metal outside the house it will not remain effective as long as indoors. But, even so, it eliminates many cleanings.

When the lacquer shows signs of failing in its task, a new coat can be put on by giving the metal a thorough cleaning with **denatured alcohol**, applied with a soft brush. This softens the lacquer when it can be soaked with hot water, after which it can be rubbed off and renewed.

The old fashioned pewter ware of our grandmother's day is extremely popular just now. It should be cleaned only with a very fine abrasive. Use either the finest grade of steel wool No. 00 with soap or a fine friction powder, when the pewter demands a drastic cleaning. Always wash it in hot soap suds after scouring and give it a final polish with a clean soft cloth. A paste of rottenstone and oil keeps clean pewter in excellent condition and with a beautiful fine gray sheen.

Nickeled **faucets** are often brass in foundation, therefore coarse abrasives of any sort will, in time, remove the plating, when there is nothing left to do but buy new or have the old faucets replated. Therefore, their best treatment is a washing only with soap suds. Keep them as dry as possible. A small stack of paper napkins kept in the bathroom medicine closet will furnish an easy means of wiping the bathroom fixtures dry in the routine of tidying up. When the nickel requires more drastic treatment use a prepared nickel polish.

Cooking utensils offer perhaps the most trying kind of metal cleaning. Stains, and burnt on food, should be removed from aluminum ware by means of fine steel wool and a fine friction soap or powder or by dry heat. Any possible scratching of the metal must be considered as secondary to the completeness of cleaning. Never use soda.

Soda water in solution is effective with enamel ware, if food has burnt on the bottom. Leave a concentrated solution in the container over night or allow it to come to a slow boil for a more rapid cleaning. Any of the friction scouring powders are a quick and excellent means of routine cleaning.

Glass ware in its common cookery usage logically comes within the scope of metal cleaning. It often requires more than the mere washing with soap and water. Fine steel wool and scouring powder will quickly remove the brown stains left when food is baked on, especially around the top of casseroles and baking dishes.

We need hardly give the experienced housekeeper any warning that metal cleaning, particularly of brass and copper, plays havoc with one's hands and fingernails. A pair of **gloves**, canvas, leather or rubber, a lemon cut in two and any good hand lotion are logically a part of the

METAL CLEANING

metal cleaning equipment. If you will include them in your kit you will be repaid both in comfort and appearance.

The Care of the Stove

Like the refrigerators, new methods of construction have made a great difference in the care that must be accorded the **kitchen range**. It used to be the practice to use black graphite or a substitute in the form of stove polish. At best the polishing was an unpleasant task and the result, while beautiful to look at, was trying to work with since the polish was so soft that it yielded up its black in the form of smootches on the worker's utensils, apron, etc.

For this reason, even for the **coal range,** I like to advise the use of a special cleansing oil adapted for such a purpose. Such a cleansing oil can be found at the hardware shops in a variety of manufactured brands. In using apply it liberally to a warm but not hot surface, wiping as dry as possible. It cleans and leaves an oil dressing that repels rust. It does not change a reddened surface to a black one and some older housekeepers, therefore, hesitate to begin its use.

Both coal and gas ranges that have had their surfaces enameled are, of course, kept in good condition merely by the use of ordinary dusting and washing but their steel lids are best treated with this same oil.

Gas stoves can be kept in excellent condition as to oven linings if such a cleansing oil is freely used It is a real

BUSINESS OF HOUSEKEEPING

rust preventive but will not correct the trouble after once rust has developed.

In storing for the winter an **oil stove** or a **gas stove** be sure that it is liberally covered with a coating of this oil. Cover with cloths or paper, to keep out the dust. And just before using wipe off all surplus and polish the stove. I have kept an oil range in service at the seashore for eight consecutive summers by such care.

And by the way oil stoves are useful only when their **burners** are kept clean. If you have the **wickless type** of oil burner keep a whisk broom hanging near it and give the burners a daily brushing. Of course, wipe up any crums or spillage left on the tray beneath the burners and give the range an occasional treatment with the cleansing oil. In the case of the **wick burner** give the wicks a daily cleaning. It is so simply accomplished, it will take but a moment; and in my case it has insured the use of the same wicks over this entire period of eight years. Fold over the forefinger a bit of soft tissue paper. Remove the inside burner cone or spreader and brush any loose match ends from the burner part. Drop the wick until it is just level with the outer rim of the container and wipe with your forefinger, using a circular motion that packs the carbon down evenly. If the wicks have been neglected it may be necessary to raise the wicks slightly and repeat this wiping, packing motion until you have a smooth layer. Never cut wicks. At the first using allow them to burn

METAL CLEANING

raggedly until enough carbon has developed to thus smooth it off and pack down. Such treatment will insure you an even blue flame with no inefficient peaks of light.

SHEETS BY SIZE

I have always been bothered by not knowing what size my sheets were when they came out of the laundry or the closet. I have now one less thing to worry me; for each sheet is marked so that I know at once whether it is narrow, medium, or wide. With a tape measure I measured every sheet I owned, and sorted them into three piles—narrow, medium, and wide. I left the narrow sheets unmarked. I marked the medium sheets with one cross in red marking cotton over the edge of the narrow hem, and I marked the wide sheets with two crosses in the same place. My sheets are now in three piles in my linen closet, and I know exactly what size sheet I am getting when I take one from the closet. What is more important, I can tell at a glance which pile the sheet belongs to, after it has been laundered.

—*Good Housekeeping Discovery.*

SAVE LEMON RIND

After using the juice of lemons, save the rinds for whitening your drainboard. Rub the inside of the rind over the board, then sprinkle with a soap cleanser. Let stand a few minutes, scrub with a brush, and wash clean. The result is well worth the effort.

—*Good Housekeeping Discovery.*

CHAPTER III

Floor Treatment and Care

PERHAPS you have floors—or a floor—that show roughness, splinters, and cracks. It is not so hopeless in your scheme of efficient housekeeping as first thought would indicate. A number of things may be done to the hopeless looking floor that will make it look well and reasonably easy to care for—two things every housekeeper looks for in **floor treatment.**

First, have you thought of **plain carpeting?** I mean of the background type. It is not expensive as carpeting goes and it can be found in all the plain neutral shades, including the browns, and it lends itself to all schemes of decorations. But someone asks, "Isn't carpeting dusty and insanitary?" Not at all, so long as our kindly friend the vacuum cleaner is available to make the cleaning dustless. Indeed the housekeeper's whole attitude toward carpeting will change, I believe, once she realizes that it is no harder to run the vacuum cleaner over an entire carpeted floor than to run it over several rugs on a bare floor.

FLOOR TREATMENT AND CARE

The greatest objection to carpeting seems to be the cost. It is not quite the lifetime investment that a well laid wood floor will prove to be. In a rented home or where first cost is more important than considerations of wear, it is a floor treatment that should be considered.

If you have no vacuum cleaner, do not consider the carpeted floor. Instead there are **wood floors** and **linoleum**. Linoleum is attractive in appearance even for living room use if you choose the neutral brown shades or tile patterns but don't make the mistake of using parquet wood patterns. They deceive no one, and in house decoration as in life it is the attempt to deceive that most offends. Buy and use **linoleum** for what it is, a smooth, sanitary, attractive, easily cleaned floor. For halls, bedrooms, nursery, porches, and all downstairs service rooms it is excellent.

Painted or stained varnished or shellacked floors are the cheapest in first cost. The cost of renewal depends upon the use and care, to say nothing of the quality of the material selected. But the real secret of a fairly good appearance and durability even in an old and splintery floor, lies, I believe, in the color—walnut brown. To be sure the cracks are still there, but no reflecting light makes the defects glaringly apparent.

First, remove with a hand plane the loose splintery pieces, but do not attempt to plane it smooth. Do not fill any cracks. I know this sounds like heresy but crack fillers never stay "put," and they never take stain like board, therefore, they lose on both counts of durability and appearance. The cracks will still be there, but you will be surprised how inconspicuous they become.

Next decide on your materials. Choose a **varnish stain** which comes ready mixed or a stain to be applied and followed by shellac or varnish. The varnish stain which comes ready mixed is easier to use, and is excellent in amateur hands, but the colors are apt to be deeper and more opaque than when a stain is used. A walnut stain over pine boards does not conceal the grain; it accents it and for that reason I like to use the two applications. Where there is no grain beauty to develop, or you can find an added advantage in the ready mixed stain varnish, use it, since there is no object in the two operations.

Color deserves a word—it is possible to select light colors for good floors of beautiful grain and smooth boards, but the worse the condition of the floor the more neutral and dark must be the color. Dark oak for medium poor floors is the very lightest color advisable. Never use mahogany stain because it is violent in color and continually invites you to look at the floor only to see its imperfections. Walnut is the best choice of all because it is neutral.

It is not too difficult to stain and varnish floors yourself. Dress for the part in knickers or bloomers that are not too full, then fasten over the knees cushion pads that are flexible enough for comfortable moving but padded enough

FLOOR TREATMENT AND CARE

to protect. Another method is to use a garden cushion and move it along as you work. Apply the stain or varnish with the grain of the wood and select a brush wide enough to do two narrow or one wider board at one sweep. Thus equipped, it is easier to do an even ''job.'' Allow each coat to dry thoroughly before applying a second. The longer a newly varnished or shellacked surface is left to harden and dry, the greater will be the return in durability.

The **waxed floor** is possibly most popular in the house that is owned, because owners are often more willing to watch the beauty of the floor develop as it does through years of actual usage. A new oak floor, even though perfectly waxed, is by no means as beautiful in appearance as this same floor will be in five years' time. The original waxing of a floor calls for nothing but some one of the many brands of **paste wax.** This must usually be softened by **turpentine,** until it can be easily rubbed into the floor. Winter application requires more turpentine than summer because the temperature tends to soften it. If no machine is available it must be applied by hand. A garden cushion will protect the knees against too much discomfort—apply liberally. There are machines now available for applying the wax as well as for polishing it and there are devices for polishing after the wax has once been applied. The first step is to apply **paste wax.** There are many good proprietary brands available. The wax must be soft in consistency but still have a body. If you find it rather hard in the can, you can soften it with **turpentine,** adding a small amount at a time until the desired consistency is obtained. When you have covered the entire floor, let it stand to permit the surface to absorb the wax and become **dry** before proceeding to the next step, which is a brushing. The floor may be brushed to work the wax into the pores of the wood as well as possible. The last step is a rubbing that gives the floor a finish or a polish if desired. Soft cloth is fitted over the brushes or a **padded polisher** is used and worked back and forth on the floor. The weight of this machine eliminates the necessity of **a** downward pressure on the part of the operator.

Routine floor care, although perhaps one of the most uninteresting of the many cares of the housekeeper, is one of the most essential, for a neglected floor will greatly detract from the room furnishings no matter how beautiful they might be.

Varnished floors may be kept polished by some one of the oil preparations; for this purpose one of the oil polish mops should be installed in a cleaning closet. Use the oil polish *very sparingly* on the **oil polish mop** once a week. The secret of perfect care of oil polished floors is that before the polish is added, the floor itself must be perfectly clean and free from dust. To use the oil polish mop to dust the floor is about as bad housekeeping as it is possible to imagine. It is a real cause for gummy floors and black corners. Use a **vacuum cleaner** *adjusted* for bare floors or a **chemical** dust mop first; then the **polish mop**, remembering that it is intended only for what its name implies—polishing and not cleaning.

Shellacked floors have a hard, brilliant, glassy, tough finish. It is best protected by a slight film of **liquid wax**. Once a week at most, some times only twice a month apply the merest suspicion of liquid wax to a cloth tied over a dry mop head and go over the floors. Thresholds and traffic areas can be treated oftener if they require it. On shellacked floors, however, do not try to rub to a polish with weights. Use a mop head with light even strokes and only until the liquid wax is evaporated to dryness. **Painted floors** should always be given a final coat of shellac or varnish and they may then be handled exactly as is the shellacked floor.

In rooms that have much use, the daily **run** with a **vacuum cleaner** is not too much whether it be rug, or carpet, to be cleaned. Especially if there is a house dog it is imperative to do this once a day. No matter what the make of vacuum cleaner selected, so long as it is approved by Good Housekeeping Institute it may be used freely, without damage to the carpets. The cleaner the carpet, the less wear and tear, for sharp grit is cut into the fabrics by the heels of the family footgear. In rooms that have not excessive use, the daily run with a **carpet sweeper,** and a weekly run with a vacuum cleaner is a better division of labor. Let your own conditions govern the use of these two invaluable tools.

The daily care of **waxed floors** is extremely simple. Use a very small amount of **softened paste wax** and the waxing machine once in two weeks. You can feel quite free to apply it on any section of the floor that dulls and seems to show need for special care. On the other hand you can use one of the liquid preparations which contains a cleansing medium and cleans and polishes the floor at one and the same time. If you choose one of these **liquid wax preparations** consistently, it is doubtful if you will ever have to apply paste wax to the floor again. In the four years of constant use in my home no second paste wax treatment has been needed. An ink stain on a waxed floor can be removed with **steel wool** and the wax finish renewed on the scoured area.

Be sure to apply liquid wax by dipping a cloth covered floor mop into the wax itself. Apply with light even strokes until the entire floor has been covered and the wax has evaporated to dryness. Polish with one of the weighted brushes, if you want the floor to have a high sheen. I never use a polishing stroke on stair treads, or what I would call danger spots, as thresholds, and "main traveled" routes to other rooms. The high polish as a border finish around a single large rug is beautiful, but in a room with a number of small light rugs, it is most inadvisable.

FLOOR TREATMENT AND CARE

It is just as important to have the floors clean before the liquid wax is applied, as before the oil polish. An excellent way to accomplish it is to use the vacuum cleaner with the bare-floor adjustment.

The over-conscientious housewife as well as many a housekeeper who learned her house care by older fashioned methods, sometimes makes the grave mistake of washing floors with soap or soap powder and water.

I think it is not too much to say that with the present day help that the manufacturers of formulas for floor care offers the housekeeper, no soap and water care is needed, provided she uses these chemical cleaning methods properly. Water is injurious to wood, because it dries it out, taking from it its natural oils and finish, leaving it in a condition ready to splinter.

Has it ever occurred to you to wonder why the floors constructed within the last few years do not show the tendency to splinter, that older fashioned homes used to do? The housekeeper then believed that only the "hard" wood floor could escape this tendency, but today soft woods are given the same floor finish and the same floor care with equally good results. No, the answer must be that today we are protecting the wood against drying out by restoring to it the oils and waxes and finish that it requires to keep it alive.

Don't scrub floors, then, unless you require it for a real germ killing purpose. If you buy a house, or rent a house that someone else has lived in, by all means have the floors washed once with strong **disinfecting materials,** but just so soon as they are dry restore to them the **oils or wax** you have removed. In just to the extent that you replace the old fashioned water treatment with this newer chemistry cleaning of floors, in just that proportion will your floor remain alive and a thing of beauty.

There are two special floors that need special mention. **Tiling** in the bathroom calls for a friction cleanser in powdered or cake form with brush and water. But here again use only enough to make the cleanser operate as a paste. Remember that the more water you put on the floor the more you will have to take up.

Use no strong solution or chemical unadvisedly, since the surface of the tile may become so roughened as to be more difficult to keep clean. The tile men themselves use muriatic acid to clean off the excessive cement. They carefully protect their hands and perform the whole job with precision, so that if such drastic cleaning is required, it is advisable to have these professionals do it. However, the occasional stain around the **toilet seats** may be removed by using a very weak solution of this same acid. So soon as the stain is removed, scrub the spot with water to which ammonia has been added.

More and more the kitchen, the porch floor, certain halls, **the** nursery, and service rooms generally are being covered

FLOOR TREATMENT AND CARE

with **linoleum.** Since the discovery that cementing the linoleum to the floor made a floor of permanent sanitation and comfort, this product has become dignified into far wider application. But its beauty and satisfaction as a floor depend very largely upon its laying and care.

Kitchen linoleum should be cared for by wiping up any spot of soil as soon as possible. For the inlaid linoleum wax is an effective finish both from the point of cost of upkeep and that of utility and beauty of appearance. The first waxing is identical with that as outlined for the wood floors and the after care is best accomplished by occasional washing when it is really needed, followed immediately by a fresh application of wax, using either the softened wax in the machine or the liquid wax as described.

Apply the liquid wax consistently once a week. Actual washing may often be put off for a period of a month, but let your own conditions govern this. In every case follow every washing with the wax application. With such treatment the linoleum remains soft and pliable, impervious to soil because its pores are so filled with wax that they repel the particles of dirt which otherwise could be ground in.

For the printed linoleum varnish is a good protective coating, but care should be taken in renewing it before it wears off at those points where the tread is greatest.

BUSINESS OF HOUSEKEEPING

HOUSEHOLD FURNISHINGS SCRAP-BOOK

Every person who is contemplating furnishing a new home has to have some sort of list, before she begins to buy the furnishings necessary. As the prices and qualities of furniture, rugs, kitchenware, and linens are numerous, the task is not so easy as it would seem. So I have found an improvised scrap-book of household furnishings of great assistance. I cut out advertisements from newspapers and magazines—especially sale advertisements showing the regular price and the sale price. I grouped my advertisements into living-room furniture, bedroom furniture, dining room furniture, kitchen furniture, rugs, linens, silver, glassware and china, kitchenware, bathroom and laundry furniture, electric appliances, and the inevitable miscellaneous, and then could compare prices and compute values. This book was meant merely for my own information and convenience, but my mother and several neighbors found occasion to make use of it, so I am persuaded it may have interest for others as well. —*Good Housekeeping Discovery.*

CHAPTER IV

Furniture Cleaning and Polishing

IT is routine care to wipe over the **woodwork of furniture** with a soft polishing cloth, then occasionally rub it down with a small amount of **furniture polish**, but wood finishes sometimes require more than that. Occasionally cleaning is necessary before the polish is applied. Therefore, as soon as you find that the usual rubbing with furniture polish does not give a clean, bright finish, try **washing with pure soap and water**. Into a gallon of warm water shave one-half cake or 3½ oz. of castile soap, then add one ounce of any bland oil such as corn, olive, cottonseed, etc. When the soap has entirely dissolved, pour into jars and label.

The solution was made up in Good Housekeeping Institute and tested carefully upon all kinds of fine furniture. It was also used upon hard-varnished finishes found on old-fashioned furniture, upon rubbed enamel, and painted furniture as well as reed and rattan. It washes them clean without harm to finish. It leaves a soft luster, but it in no sense takes the place of the usual furniture polish. The new rubbed-down and waxed finish of mahogany and walnut, however, will need no further polish after their soft luster is restored.

But possibly all of you do not know just how to apply furniture polish to get the best results. The secret lies in the following method: Pour into a glass jar two tablespoonfuls of any one of the furniture polishes that you like best to use, but pour it immediately out again. In the empty jar place a square of velveteen or chamois or even Italian silk, although the two former give better results. Cheesecloth does not absorb quite so uniformly. Leave the cloth in the empty jar for a day or two before you attempt to use it. It is surprising how the polish penetrates the fabric—in small amounts, to be sure, but uniformly and in sufficient quantity to polish without leaving any traces of the polish itself. And that, after all, is what we wish in furniture cleaning. Until the wood needs actual washing, use this cloth, then, for the routine dusting. It will dust and polish at the same time. It is adaptable for use on the piano or on any other highly finished wood as well as the whole gamut of veneer finishes.

White spots and "fog" are often a bug-bear. These spots are especially apt to come after a vase of flowers or a glass has been standing on the side-table. The so-called "fog" or whitish bloom found on furniture is a less acute symptom of exactly the same disease, and both are caused by a reaction between water and the varnish in the furniture

FURNITURE CLEANING AND POLISHING

finish. With a table top treated solely with either oil or wax in the now popular rubbed-down finish, these water spots cannot occur. They are especially common in the so-called "gift" furniture of mahogany that is too often carelessly finished. The remedy is simple. Wipe over with a cloth wrung as dry as possible from weak ammonia water; then polish with whatever furniture polish you use. The ammonia in the water simply restores the color, and the polish is needed to restore the finish.

Wicker and reed furniture present a problem in themselves. A stiff brush and the cleaning solution whose formula I have given constitute the best treatment. Either paint, stain, or varnish can be used to restore color. If you wish a light stain, thin either the oak or walnut, and you will get the protection the varnish affords to the wicker, with the new look which many housekeepers enjoy in wicker furniture.

The painted furniture in both rubbed enamel and plain finishes responds perfectly to the cleaning solution. A very small amount of furniture polish may be used afterward if desired. It possibly lessens the tendency for an oily film of soft coal dust to stick on the wood finish. Be sure that you do not use too much, however.

Papered walls are impractical to attempt to clean beyond wiping them over with a dry soft wool cloth or mop. But an occasional defacing grease spot can be treated with one of the commercial wall paper cleaners.

BUSINESS OF HOUSEKEEPING

Woodwork and wall surfaces also act as catch-alls for the pest of soil. Both woodwork and wall surfaces, provided the latter are painted, can be truly restored to cleanliness by washing, but there is a right and wrong way to do this, and success depends upon using the right way.

Whatever the surface to be treated, whether wall or wood, the method of actual washing is identical. Success depends upon using the smallest possible amount of water. Wring the cloth as dry as possible. Place your left hand at one end of the cloth, your right hand at the other, palms up. Use the left hand as the wringing lever, and the cloth can be wrung to wringer dryness. Use friction soap; any variety will prove satisfactory. When a small amount of friction powder is applied to the cloth, use an up-and-down and never a circular motion. Clean only a small section at a time and dry immediately with a clean dry cloth. This method is proof against streaks.

PUTTING AWAY SCREENS

Very soon we shall all be storing away the window screens until next summer. Perhaps every housewife does not know that it is possible to buy at a hardware store duplicate sets of numbers on brass tack-heads. Tack one of these numbers on a window frame and the corresponding number on the screen belonging to the window. Then there will be no trouble next spring in fitting the screens, as you will know instantly where each one belongs.

—*Good Housekeeping Discovery.*

FURNITURE CLEANING AND POLISHING

TO RENEW WHITE WINDOW SHADES

While having my bathroom enameled, I remarked to the painter that I should be most happy to discover some way of making the white window shades fresh and clean again, as they had become soiled from long use. Immediately he came to my rescue, removed the shades, took them out into the garage, and hung them against the wall. Then he gave the shades a coat of flat white paint, and when they were dry, he put green paint on the other side, and now the shades look like new.
—*Good Housekeeping Discovery.*

TO KEEP THE HANDS WHITE

Although I know that constant use of lemon juice on my hands after peeling vegetables will keep them clean and white, I never seem to have the lemons handy. So I have bought a liquid soap container, and fastened it above my sink, and keep some lemon juice in it all the time. It is always easy to tip it and get a few drops every time I wash my hands while cooking. Of course, the use of cold-cream or some lotion is necessary after washing, to keep the hands soft. —*Good Housekeeping Discovery.*

CHAPTER V

Closet and Storeroom Care

TIMES have changed. Before the comparatively recent days of perfected househeating every housekeeper had a **cold storeroom** at least for winter use: there hung in orderly rows or packed away in newspapers and moth repellents she felt reasonably safe so far as furs, extra blankets, winter woolens, etc., were concerned.

But today it is not possible even in winter to forget the moth and the deadly Buffalo bug. They are no longer a seasonal pest. They are an all the year round duty.

Unquestionably the **commercial cold storage** represents safety to valuable garments and a minimum expense. Even if you have to ship them some distance for this storage it will repay you during the summer months, but much of the damage I find is done in those between season months when one hardly dares to be without the warmth that may be needed but once or even not at all. In spring and in fall perhaps the maximum of effort is needed on the part of the housekeeper to protect her possessions.

Closet care, both routine and occasional, becomes a real issue. Fortunately architects are building more closets and more specialized closets into our homes. They are endeavoring to make it as easy as possible for us to control the moth pest. For instance, the linen closet is no longer a novelty, but even if you are without one its convenience and real economy can be enjoyed at small expense, if you will build a set of more or less shallow shelves depending on the space at your command. Use any convenient wall. Then enclose them with doors. Oftentimes a second bathroom door can be blocked up and thus used. Look around you and see if your home does not afford the necessary wall space and twenty-inch depth for the shelves.

Make the upper shelf the blanket shelf, and therefore line it throughout—ceiling, walls and shelf floor—with heavy sheets of any so-called "moth proofed" paper. As a further precaution one of the liquid insecticides should be sprayed thoroughly into the blankets and wool puffs to be stored on the shelf. Use this treatment twice a year at least or oftener if a flying moth gives warning of trouble. Blanket care in summer is more of a question. They may be cleaned either by washing or dry cleaning and stored in cedar chests or trunks. On the other hand if they can be kept thoroughly sprayed they should be safe at home even on their usual shelves.

Every individual in a family should have his or her own closet where they should be held responsible for the simple routine care of hanging up garments and the orderly arrangement of shoes, hats and smaller traveling gear. Shoes need a word of mention because they are often the cause of an untidy appearance. As a matter of fact properly cared for shoes last so much longer and look so much trimmer that it is not only good housekeeping but good thrift to properly care for them. Occasionally one finds a closet properly equipped with a **shoe carrier** but if you do not have one, any carpenter at comparatively small cost can build you a set of sloping shelves. Kept on these shelves with shoe trees in each pair one can expect the longest possible period of service.

There is no better arrangement either for men's or women's garments than the **pole** suspended from the walls of the closet, from which almost a limitless number of garment hangers may be hung. Be careful that this pole is changed in height in the children's closets so that it becomes easy for them to learn the tidy habit of hanging up their own garments. Even a closet that is too shallow for the ordinary coat hanger can be so utilized if you will purchase children's smaller hangers or chop off the larger ones at each end to the necessary width. A coat hanger does not have to reach so far into the shoulders of the garment, for instance, in order to hang properly. Be sure to sandpaper

CLOSET AND STOREROOM CARE

carefully and then wind with a rough but not wool fabric as corduroy.

Men's clothes are far more difficult to care for and protect than the average woman's. Possibly because they are almost, if not quite, all wool, and also because an occasional grease spot often missed in cleaning offers the most attractive of meals to our enemy, the moth. Perhaps other housekeepers can get along without all of my precautions, but they have proved real protection so I pass them on. First, every closet holding garments has its lining of cedarized paper. Second, every closet has its monthly cleaning and the garments are sprayed with a good insecticide. And finally every closet is equipped with the commercial **moth proof bags** into which seasonal clothes may be placed after being cleaned. For the convenience of the user they are not removed to another closet. Since using this method I have not even had the tiniest moth hole appearing in any garment.

And that brings us to the question of **storage.** What shall we keep, what is wise thrift to give away or otherwise dispose of? It used to be thrift to maintain "piece bags." Today they must be moth proof or not at all. It used to be thrift to store a garment with little possibility of another use. It was "too good to throw away." Today all that is changed. Every garment, every blanket, every puff that is not worth the cost or the effort or both of thorough

BUSINESS OF HOUSEKEEPING

cleaning is not worth storing. It will prove too costly in its damage to other garments to pay.

Today with a washing machine installed in a laundry it is a simple matter to wash **woolen blankets and wool puffs.** There need be no special cleaner's bills for these. And by the way it is in the occasional curtain and blanket washing that most women have an added feeling of thankfulness for that washing machine installed in their laundry.

In preparing **suits and overcoats,** either send them to the tailor for his cleaning and pressing or you may do the work at home. Choose the cool laundry to work in and an ironing board with an old cover, because it will be stained and useless after this task. For cleaning use one of the non-inflammable cleaning fluids or naphtha, benzine, or a good grade of gasoline made non-inflammable. Ask your druggist to add enough carbon tetrachloride to make these otherwise dangerous cleaning fluids safe. And by the way both the gasoline and tetrachloride are strong moth repellents.

Connect the vacuum cleaner and with the hand tool go over each garment; pay special attention to fur collars and spots of soil. Then dip a brush into the fluid and brush the entire garment with strong even strokes. Again pay especial attention to all spots and to the seams of the garment. And as soon as each garment is completed place it in its protecting bag before the fumes have had an opportunity to dissipate.

CLOSET AND STOREROOM CARE

Finally, just a word about the home that is really infested with **moths**. It was my unhappy experience to purchase a home in which this pest was appallingly present. I could protect the individual garment and the individual blanket but moths were still flying around the house and moths were still breeding in the walls. All this, in spite of the fact that every inch of the house was given three or more coats of paint before we even moved in.

It was not until the commercial exterminator was called in with his gas treatment that the house was entirely rid of the pest, and I believe it to be a good procedure, when going into a home that has been occupied by other people, to have this fumigating process done, irrespective of the painting and redecorating that may be planned for. It is a task that must be done by skilled workers but it does not require an undue time. While they ask for only four hours before it is safe and comfortable to use the house, it is wiser, I believe, to spend one night out of the house unless the task is done in the winter months when it is much easier to obtain fresh currents of air through the rooms.

CHAPTER VI

Cellar Care and Cleanliness

NEARLY every housekeeper has asked herself the question: "How much care should a good housekeeper accord the **cellar?**" Is it a daily, a weekly, a monthly or a semi-annual affair, this of cellar cleaning. According to the primer of housework, the modern self-respecting cellar calls for a casual weekly attention, to be sure, but it is the semi-annual cleaning after all that keeps it sweet and clean and healthful.

The weekly care calls only for a general tidying. Dispose of newspapers and magazines that may have accumulated. I have two capacious baskets. Both newspapers and magazines are placed flat in their respective baskets when they are no longer required above stairs. No second handling is required when they are taken away to their final destination of hospital, Salvation Army headquarters, or junk man.

Dispose promptly of broken articles consigned to the cellar because they are out of sight. Reclaim them at once if there

CELLAR CARE AND CLEANLINESS

is a possibility of repair. But chop up or burn up ruthlessly if there is no hope of rescue. Most cellars are untidy rather than unclean and solely because the cellar is used, as the attic, for broken or discarded furnishings.

See that the **fire wood** for the grate is an orderly pile. Use a bin for the kindling wood for all fires. You can easily build it with one or two three to four foot high partitions. Oftener, only one will be needed for the wall of the coal bin can be used for the other. In the fall, the ash cans must be given an appraising glance. Small ones and many of them are best, for then they are not too great a task of strength in handling. If father or son does the work, a two wheeled ash can truck will prove as useful a tool as mother's vacuum cleaner is upstairs.

In most cellars, there is a **tool room** sacred to the masculine members of the family. I would leave this untidy.

But the **storeroom** deserves a word. Many housekeepers are finding it impossible to keep food supplies purchased in large quantities from molestation by mice or rats. The best solution I have found is a series of swing shelves suspended from each other and from the ceiling, and preferably in the center of the room. Be sure you leave not a scrap of food within reach and even in a waterfront city, they may leave for less hungry quarters. Of course, canned goods, in tin, can be stored with impunity on wall shelves, but glass jars must go on the swing shelves with the rest of the supplies, because the hungry rat can break them.

BUSINESS OF HOUSEKEEPING

During both the fall and winter months, the **cellar floor** is flushed with water which is swept down the center drain with a strong, plain, old-fashioned broom, a tool that cannot be dispensed with in a housekeeper's régime. This keeps down the ash dust and freshens the whole house. In summer I find no necessity for this washing. But in both winter and summer, the cellar stairs must be washed each week. Now it happens that that particular task is the most difficult to parcel out in a two-maid household. Therefore, I always list it in the work very plainly before engaging a servant and thereby save a disagreeable interview later.

The semi-annual care of the cellar is a spring or fall affair. Oftentimes, the work can be accomplished just as well once a year. It all depends upon the amount of traffic the cellar has to bear. But either in the spring or the fall, a coat of whitewash should be applied to both cellar and furnace. If in the spring, be sure that it is late enough for no further emergency fires.

First of all, have the **furnace** cleaned of its clogging soot, the pipes taken down, given a coat of asphalt paint and stored away in paper for use in the fall. If it has not been done, it is a wise move to cover the heater with thick layers of an asbestos composition, in the form especially prepared for this furnace use. Then treat it like the rest of the cellar with a coat of whitewash, using the asphalt paint to give the metal trim a glossy coat of black. In this particular cellar, the furnace man "arm" installed at the side of

CELLAR CARE AND CLEANLINESS

the furnace proved so real a convenience that I pass it on. Upon it, within convenient reach, are hung the tools needed for the task of furnace care.

Just a word in regard to the **whitewashing**. I carry my taste for color right down into the cellar and add enough tinted cold water paint to the whitewash so that I have old ivory on the walls and coal and wood bin partition. It is no more expensive and I do assure you that it is far more sightly than the glaring white.

By the way, if the **coal bins** are to be filled with coal some time during the summer, you may prefer to delay the whitewashing until the early fall after the winter supply is stored. This is exactly as satisfactory a procedure, provided there is no tendency to dampness in the cellar. Indeed there may be localities where the coat of whitewash will be needed both spring and fall. It has a tendency to absorb moisture and keep the cellar dry and therefore is a matter of health quite as much as cleanliness to attend to it.

Finally, not a word has been said in this book as to who should take care of the cellar, but the logical shoulders to assume the task are those of the son of the house. By all means, let the boys have a sense of responsibility for the cleanliness and tidiness of this part of the house.

CHAPTER VII

Spring Renovating

THERE is not a housekeeper but welcomes the first signs that the time has, at last, come to open the house and to make ready for the months of **outdoor housekeeping.** The time to do this must vary in this wide country of ours, but the tasks themselves remain fairly constant.

With the first breath of mildness, then, take off the **storm windows and doors** if you have them. Go over them carefully for lights that need replacing or reputtying, and for the repainting that secures longer life. Store them away safely and carefully. Be sure that each one is tagged with its window number. These numbers in duplicate come now in thumb tack form and can be easily applied. Time and patience are saved by this practice, when they are installed in the fall. The house equipped with weatherstripping will, of course, not require this task. But in both cases **screens** should be installed early before there can be even a suggestion of a fly. The house that installs screens early and takes them down late is the flyless house in real fly time. And just a word about screens. If you must replace, this year, by all means do it by screening the

SPRING RENOVATING

entire window. Once tried, I am sure you will never go back to the half screen window that used to satisfy us.

Lawn furniture, if of iron, may need a furbishing up. Wash the furniture first and follow with a **liquid wax polish,** rubbing to restore the jet black appearance. Even repainting is not a difficult job because it can be done on the first glorious out of door days when any task that takes us outside is a welcome one. Use jet black paint with the dull finish. Even if the chairs are of wood, try this same jet black treatment. I believe you will like it better than either the green or natural wood that is so commonly used.

Porch furniture, if of reed or wicker or rattan, can be safely scrubbed if it really needs it. Finish by rubbing with **furniture polish** if you wish to retain the natural color. The furniture polish treatment should be given alone, if the furniture does not require scrubbing. **Willow furniture** is more difficult to clean. It never looks "as good as new" after washing, so it is much better to stain or paint it. An excellent two toned effect is not difficult to obtain even by unskilled home painting. Choose any desired colors: orange, green or red with black; or "tipcart" blue with light oak varnish make excellent combinations. First paint the entire chair with the brilliant color, and before it dries at all wipe off with a cloth as much of the color as you can, leaving it only in crevices, etc. Let it dry thoroughly and then apply the top coat, using the second and more neutral color and painting lightly to touch only the

BUSINESS OF HOUSEKEEPING

wiped over unpainted surface. If a light stain or varnish is used for this second coat not so much care is needed in the final painting. Re-cover the **cushions** to blend with your new color scheme and you will have new furniture for summer use.

If the **porch floors** are of wood and you use them as rooms by all means cover with **linoleum** cemented down, and waxed. It will save you untold work. Choose the large tile patterns; red pointed with black; gray pointed with red, or the black and white block pattern. All of these are excellent for porch use. But if the porch floors **are** cement here is a brand new treatment that will make them as smooth as tile and as easily cared for. If the cement is of the usual grayish pink tint, no color need be used. Simply **shellac**; where there is much wear three coats are none too many. If the cement is plain gray and you wish a color use cement paint, tile red or any other color you choose, instead of the shellac. In either case finish with **paste wax** applied warm, and thinned with only enough **turpentine** to allow it to be handled. Be sure that you do not make the paste too thin. This waxing deepens the original pinkish color to a tile red. The after care of the floor consists only in **dust mopping** and a weekly polish with a little **liquid wax or paste wax** applied with a polisher. The floor requires no scrubbing.

Rugs and carpets are always a spring consideration. The past years have been especially hard on both **rugs and**

SPRING RENOVATING

hangings because of the soft coals commonly used for fuel. Unquestionably many housekeepers may have to resort to more drastic methods than usual. But today rugs, even Oriental rugs, can be washed and cleaned safely, but it should be done by skilled hands. Most cities and some towns have carpet renovators, and even if the rugs must be shipped for some distance it is wise to use these expert rug cleaners. The cost is not prohibitive especially if you store the rugs during the summer months. If it is impossible to take advantage of professional work you can try washing them at home. Use only the best of neutral soaps and a new scrubbing brush that is not too coarse. Lay the rug on the floor, use a garden cushion to protect the knees and scrub a small area at a time. Rinse and wipe dry. Do not use a circular scrubbing motion. The greatest difficulty lies in producing perfectly even cleansing. But with care excellent results are possible.

I know of no better way to make a house more comfortable in summer and at the same time lessen housework than to pack away the **winter hangings** and cover overstuffed furniture with **washable covers**. If you will at the same time pack away all but the very necessary silver together with the brasses and bric-a-brac you will make the rooms look bigger and cooler and more restful, and at the same time simplify your own care. Even so simple a thing as the use of glass candlesticks instead of those that require polishing, as silver or mahogany, has an influence in light-

BUSINESS OF HOUSEKEEPING

ening summer work. And when fall comes you will enjoy them all the more upon their reappearance.

Next comes the task of packing away **winter garments,** blankets and wools generally. Don't forget to leave out enough wool covers to serve all the beds for that occasional cool night we always have in summer. I find that the **wool filled puff or comfort** proves the best selection because its cotton or silk cover does not look so warm as even a light wool blanket and the beds can still have their appearance of summer dress and ready comfort. **Wool underwear** cleaned and repaired can be stored in cedar chests or wrapped in mothproof paper or bag in closet or dresser. **Blankets** also if newly cleaned can be similarly stored. But unwashable garments, especially **men's suits,** should be cleaned first and thoroughly, because moths first attack spots of soil. The cleaning may be done at home or by a professional. Directions were given for this cleaning on page 104. Then immediately pack them or have them packed with a generous quantity of any of the pungent moth preventives, camphor, naphthaline, moth balls, etc. Use either boxes or the mothproof bags. Remember that the task of storing clothes against the ravages of moths, etc., is much more difficult in the spring than in the fall. Even though our superheated houses have made the moth an all year round pest it nevertheless is far more dangerous in summer.

SPRING RENOVATING

On this account it is excellent routine in this spring season to use a good **insecticide** and sprayer all over the house, in closets and servants' quarters especially. Make its use a part of the "spring cleaning" given each year.

At this time it is just as well to look over the **awnings.** There are two things to note about the newer awnings. First, is their simplicity for they no longer need be made with sides that shut out the breeze. Instead they consist of a single piece of awning duck without any sides and supported on the usual awning frame. The second point of interest lies in the material, for a very heavy canvas duck is now used painted green on top and pure white beneath. It is the most expensive awning fabric but repays its first cost in durability, for it can be renewed each year with a fresh coat of paint that protects the fabric as well as improves the appearance. The awnings never look faded, never look old. But provided the awning material is heavy enough to hold the paint there can be no objection to painting any faded but still strong awning fabric. Don't try it, however, on awnings with side pieces, and if you do try it, wait until the awnings can be hung so that the drying can be accomplished as they are stretched taut.

CHAPTER VIII

Seasonal House-Cleaning

EVEN though the newer housekeeping is founded on the principle of keeping clean rather than making clean nevertheless there is a freshness of atmosphere and a real cheer about the newly cleaned room that makes most of us housekeepers hesitate to discard the old system of house-cleaning even though it entails an occasional upheaval of the household routine.

In the following outline the work is spread over a period of two weeks allowing a Wednesday of each week for the day of recreation. The time may be lengthened to suit a larger house. The scheme so plans the work on the other days that the cleaning need not occupy the entire day.

MONDAY: clean attic.

TUESDAY: clean linen and clothes closets, bureau and chiffoniers.

THURSDAY: clean downstairs clothes closet, linen closet, and china closet, with silver and china.

FRIDAY: clean half the upstairs rooms.

SATURDAY: clean bathroom.

MONDAY: clean balance of upstairs rooms.

TUESDAY: clean half downstairs rooms.

THURSDAY: clean balance of downstairs rooms.

FRIDAY: clean kitchen.

SATURDAY: clean cellar.

SEASONAL HOUSE-CLEANING

The **attic** is the logical place to start. Because many of us have a tendency to store here **clothes** that are not good enough to wear but are too good to throw away; it is indeed wise to look these over and get rid of everything for which you have no immediate use. Reserve only those which you feel are of sufficient value to warrant an outlay for cleaning. Have them cleaned and pack them away as carefully as your newer clothes, in **mothproof chests**. As the attic will be dusty, rather than actually dirty, go over the floor with a **vacuum cleaner**, then wipe it with a small amount of water, and plenty of **disinfectant**. All **closets used for storerooms** are the next logical step. Each **drawer** in closet, dresser, or chiffonier should be taken out and rapped sharply on the bottom with a small hammer since these are the places where tiny insect eggs lodge to hatch out in warm weather. Each drawer should be thoroughly sprayed with a moth **preventive**, after washing out with warm water to which **household ammonia** and any good disinfectant has been added. When dry renew with clean fresh **lining paper**. Don't forget to empty completely and actually clean each closet and storeroom. See that the **walls** are brushed down, the tops of **ledges** washed and the **shelves** taken out if removable. One tiny insect egg left under a loose shelf may cause much damage and work. Moth damage can be prevented if after washing the shelves a moth preventive is used in one of the efficient **spraying machines**. But spray thoroughly!

BUSINESS OF HOUSEKEEPING

With bureau drawers and store closets finished, begin with bookcases, writing desk, sewing machine drawers, medicine cabinets, blacking cases and utility boxes.

Books and bookcases are neither easy nor pleasant to clean for the books must all be removed and they are heavy to handle. It ranks with the china closet as one of the most trying of housecleaning tasks. Remove all the books to a porch, open each one in several places and beat lightly with a small bamboo beater or a brand new velvet edged fly swatter. With a clean cloth, dust the edges and wipe the books before replacing in the cleaned bookcase.

In cleaning the **china closet** all dishes should be removed, washed and dried. The cut glasses should be washed in hot soapy water and rinsed in clear water to which ammonia has been added. Dry on soft linen and polish with a piece of paper.

Room cleaning has a procedure all its own. First take down all **curtains and portières**. Wash, dust and remove **ornaments, books, pictures**, etc. Next clean the **rug or carpet** with a vacuum cleaner. Place the **portières** on the clean rug and run the vacuum cleaner over them until they are clean. Roll up the portières as soon as clean and hang outdoors to air thoroughly. Give the **rugs** a final cleaning and roll them up. If a bedroom, **mattresses** may be put directly on the floor and the vacuum cleaner used on them or the cleaning tool may be used, paying especial attention to all tufting. Overstuffed furniture is best

SEASONAL HOUSE-CLEANING

cleaned with the attachment. Wipe down the **walls** with a clean wool mop covered with cheesecloth. Use a brush on the **radiators** and a dust mop on all woodwork. Brush up the dust on the floor with a soft floor brush or use the vacuum cleaner and finish with a wax or oil mop. **Wood trim** if painted should be cleaned with a damp cloth and friction powder. If of mahogany or any stained wood finish clean and polish only with furniture polish—being very careful to rub until perfectly dry. Next polish the **furniture** and replace carpets and portières unless they are to be stored for the summer.

It is possible that the **vacuum cleaning** of rug or carpet may not be sufficiently drastic treatment. The past season especially has been hard on rugs and hangings because of the soft coal so widely used for fuel. Today rugs, even Oriental ones, can be washed and cleaned safely. But it should be done by skilled hands. Most cities and some towns have **carpet renovating firms** and even if the rugs must be shipped for some distance it is wise to use these expert rug cleaners for expensive rugs.

CHAPTER IX

Safe Procedure in Closing a House

OCCASIONALLY emergency makes it necessary to hastily turn the key in the lock and leave a house with all save the actual necessities left undone, but the routine of leaving a home for a summer or winter stay allows of everything to be accomplished that is at all necessary, provided the housekeeper has planned and wisely made a list to be checked off as accomplished.

Procedure for the two seasons has only one variation. If the house is to be left in winter **the water** must be removed from the system, **every pipe** should be drained and the **heating system** of hot water or even steam should also be completely drained and the **traps** treated with glycerine.

While in summer there is a bit more worry from the question of moths, nevertheless in either season **moth prevention** is a real problem for moths thrive vigorously under such conditions of undisturbed quiet.

SAFE PROCEDURE IN CLOSING A HOUSE

It is wise, therefore, to send out of the house any **fur coats** and any **fur pieces,** to be stored by a reliable furrier in cold storage. **Outer garments of** wool should be vacuum cleaned and packed away in mothproof bags and cedar chests. **Blankets** should be washed or vacuum cleaned and hung in the open air before wrapping in mothproof paper. Frankly, the secret of adequate storage as a protection against moths cannot too often be repeated: garments must be absolutely clean for this will mean they are free of moth eggs. Second, the storage place must also be free of all traces of moths, and finally the storage place must be so sealed that moths will not be able to enter. It is an advantage, of course, to have these storage places so treated with sufficient repellant material distasteful to the flying moth as to prevent to some extent their entering.

As a protection against fading and dust, clean and store window **draperies, portières** and other **hangings. Washable curtains** should be laundered but put away unironed. Clean **sofa cushions** and wrap them in paper and store them in chests.

Silk lamp shades should be brushed or cleaned with the vacuum cleaner tool and wrapped in tissue paper; **parchment shades** should be wiped off and wrapped.

Overstuffed furniture should be thoroughly sprayed with a commercial moth killer and then covered with slip covers. **Wicker furniture** should be covered because it is most difficult to clean, once it becomes dusty. Old sheets or even

BUSINESS OF HOUSEKEEPING

newspaper may be used by tying with twine or by fastening with surgeon's tape around arms and legs. If, however, the house is closed each season, it is wiser to make simple inexpensive slip covers.

Cover all **lighting fixtures** with newspaper for fly specks are practically impossible to remove. Pack away bric-a-brac, candelabra, etc. Take off table runners, doilies, bureau scarfs. In the bedrooms strip the beds of all coverings and cover mattresses and pillow cases with clean sheets. It is wise to put several layers of paper between the mattress and the spring if it is not of the box type, in order to protect the mattress from dampness that may cause the metal spring to rust.

It goes without saying that **silver, jewelry and legal papers** should not be left in the house. Silver chests, special silver cases, in the form of cardboard boxes, or canton flannel cases should be used for storing silver. If you make the flannel cases yourself choose a color other than pure white, because the sulphur in the bleach will cause the silver to tarnish. Make one of these for each large piece of silver, while for the flat silver use straight lengths with pockets for individual pieces. Mark each case with its contents for ease in checking up on your return or in finding the desired articles.

Many housekeepers forget to plan wisely with regard to **food**. Plan menus ahead of time with the idea of using up perishable foods. The staples such as salt, sugar and

SAFE PROCEDURE IN CLOSING A HOUSE

flour, will keep, provided you have the right containers. They must be kept dry. **Metal containers** are best because they are both moisture-proof and vermin-proof. Dispose of every bit of food which you cannot properly store. Take everything out of the **refrigerator** and clean it thoroughly. Plug up the **drain** if it leads outdoors. Leave a refrigerator only in a dry place. And have all the doors swung open. Treat the **kitchen range** generously with stove oil to prevent its rusting. Use the same treatment for **iron fireplace fittings**.

GUARD AGAINST ANY POSSIBILITY OF FIRE

Leave no chemically prepared dusters and oil-treated mops and floor cloths in the house. Mice will gnaw on **matches** when there is nothing more attractive: as a safeguard store all matches in a tin box and label.

Dampness in the home can do much damage so make a careful survey of the basement and cellar to see that nothing which might be affected by moisture is left. It may not be feasible to remove the washing and ironing machine to the first floor because of their size. Cover the **metal parts** with stove oil, then make covers for them, preferably from oilcloth. Before putting these covers on, be sure that the machines are dry and well oiled and greased. All unprotected metal parts should be oiled with any good lubricating oil. Coat the shoe of the ironing machine generously with wax. Release the tension of the wringer

BUSINESS OF HOUSEKEEPING

roll, and should the washing machine have a wooden cylinder, remove it and store it on the first floor.

Remove the pipe from the furnace to the chimney at least so far as the section of the pipe connected to the chimney flue is concerned, for this is most susceptible to rust. Cover the **flue opening** with one of the stops to be purchased in the hardware shop, or it may be filled with paper. The same precaution should be taken with a **coal range** in the kitchen. **Fireplaces** should be inspected to make sure that all their dampers are closed. **Water and gas** should be shut off at the main inlets, usually near the meters in the cellar. This overcomes any possibility of a leak. Into all **traps** should be poured a cupful of sweet oil. This will prevent the water evaporating and thus allowing unpleasant-smelling sewer gas to enter the house. Notify the company to disconnect the **electric current.** If the house is to remain unoccupied for a period of months it is advisable to request that the main fuses be removed by the electric company. For a stay of a few weeks you yourself can remove the fuses in the individual circuits in the house. Bear in mind, however, that the house must be in darkness until the fuses are replaced and send notification of return to the power company in ample time.

Locks need only a mention. See that all window and door locks are in perfect repair and the keys are accessible.

In conclusion it is not wise to call attention by the outside appearance of the house to the fact that every one is

SAFE PROCEDURE IN CLOSING A HOUSE

away. Don't pull down the shades and close the blinds. The house which presents an inhabited rather than a deserted appearance will be least conspicuous to those having a casual malicious intent. This does not hold good, however, if the house is to be unoccupied for several months. In this case boarding the windows protects the window panes and keeps out much of the sunlight, thus preventing the fading of wall coverings. An excellent idea for the housekeeper who closes her house every summer is to make a set of inexpensive **cheesecloth curtains**. They lend a neat appearance to the exterior of the house, obscure the view from outdoors and tell no tales of absentee owner.

SECTION V

In the Laundry

Chapter I—Plan and Location

Chapter II—Equipment, Choice and Installation

Chapter III—Washing Formulas
- Soaps and Soap Compounds
- Softeners
- Blues and Tints
- Starches and Starching

Chapter IV—Laundry Methods
- The Chemistry of Washing
- The Routine of the Family Wash
- The Removal of Stains
- Sprinkling and Folding
- Washing Silks and Woolens
- Fitting the Baby's Wash into the House Routine

CHAPTER I

Plan and Location

A WELL equipped **laundry** will prove a real investment showing definite money return to your budget wherever the laundry work is assumed by paid workers: whether inside or outside the house. Its advantage to the housekeeper who does her own work while different in kind is no less obvious.

Installment purchase of this type of household equipment has a special fitness. I am well aware that such purchasing has received a bad name and I agree that save within narrow limits it should not be resorted to by the thrifty. The test I believe lies in the answers to the questions: Is it an investment returning its purchase price in work accomplished or is it a luxury whose first cost I could not possibly assume? Ask yourself the second question: Can I pay for this equipment out of money that in any case is to be spent to accomplish the work it claims to do? With an affirmative answer to both of these questions, the sound business policy of the method becomes apparent. Again in this same expenditure, the **washing machine,** the

ironing machine, and some form of **quick dryer** should all three be provided for. Three hundred to six hundred dollars will be ample to purchase and properly install all three machines. With any single one of them, certain gains in convenience, time, and quality of work are to be expected; but it is when all three of them are in harmonious operation that one obtains the maximum results. It then becomes possible to dovetail ironing and washing periods, with no delay on stormy days waiting for the slow drying of the clothes. With all of them in operation a paid worker's time is fully utilized irrespective of weather conditions.

If you can choose the **location of your laundry** you are indeed happy. You will never regret incorporating it on the ground floor adjacent to the kitchen. This can be done even in small houses by sacrificing enough kitchen and pantry space to enlarge the rear entrance hall into a serviceable laundry. Moreover, a unit system of **kitchen cabinet** with auxiliary **wall cabinets** is now furnished in a number of wood and metal constructions, and they furnish a far more efficient kitchen substitute for the old fashioned pantry.

Unconsciously better care is taken of machinery when installed on this upper floor. But of even more importance, is the greater convenience in working if you do it yourself and the greater convenience in overseeing if you hire it done. *F*inally there is greater protection to both machines

PLAN AND LOCATION

and linen, since the dust and dirt incidental to the house heating plant is a really big item in laundry work.

An ideal solution when ground space permits is the tiny laundry building built adjacent to the **drying yard** and with the whole trellised to have a real landscape value. In this case the **laundry stove** acts as **heating plant** for both workroom and dryer. With generous windows, carefully selected equipment and attractive surroundings this particular building accomplishes the entire laundry of a big family of adults and children, with no grumbling at the generous washes sent out from the house.

Many of our older houses have large laundries and oftentimes they are dark and in the basement. But their spacious dimensions make it possible to easily install all three of the large pieces of laundry equipment, and with plenty of artificial light and a generous provision for convenience outlets, such a laundry may be made into a convenient and efficient room. Plan the arrangement so that as nearly as possible the clothes are routed soiled from **clothes chute** or **laundry hampers** to the **sorting table,** thence to stain removal, thence to washing, rinsing, bluing, starching, and drying, by progressive steps towards the outer door and the drying yard, or drying machine. In the same way they should come in, dry, and progress again through the several stages of sorting, mending, sprinkling, ironing, airing and packing into hampers toward the linen room and personal bureaus of the family.

BUSINESS OF HOUSEKEEPING

The combination **kitchen and laundry** is a common provision by the architect of many small houses. It is probably the least desirable location for laundry work, but even here a little care will insure good results. Wherever and whatever the laundry is I do want to accent the necessity for isolating the laundry work as much as possible from the handling of food and the utensils used in preparing and serving it. If you wash in such a combination room, then, keep the **laundry tools**, utensils, and reagents in their own special place. There should be no temptation to borrow the **vegetable kettle** for the making of starch. **Laundry spoons** should be kept only for laundry use.

Frankly I cannot but wonder at that architect who provides the housekeeper with this combination kitchen-laundry and then offers her double dining facilities through a dining-room and an additional breakfast nook. Yes, he even adds a porch dining-room, oftentimes, to the house he deems too small for an honest laundry.

A small **kitchen cabinet** or set of shelves is excellent for storing the laundry supplies in the kitchen. In the case of the kitchen cabinet **the enameled metal top** is ideal for the stain and starch work and for sprinkling the clothes. Store the soaps, compounds and soap jellies, water softeners, bluings, tints and soap dyes on the **shelves**. Clothespins and bag with the lines can be put away in the deep drawer. In the **cabinet** proper are stored the starch and stain kettles.

CLOTHES-POSTS IN THE BACK YARD

I do my own washing, and when I moved into a lovely new home, I dreaded to put up clothes-posts, because we had a very beautiful yard. Finally, I put up posts with crosspieces on the order of a trellis, not too wide, and at the top I put a wider one of a two-by-four dimension, wide enough to take a line at each end without making them too close together. On this two-by-four trellis I put large, non-rustable hooks, painted the whole a dull green, and then put an attractive home-made bird-house on the top. I planted flowering beans, clematis, honeysuckle, etc., at the base of these posts, and they are lovely.

—Good Housekeeping Discovery.

CHAPTER II

Equipment, Choice and Installation

THE **walls** of the laundry may be of a hard plaster with a hard washable oil paint finish in any light color. The yellows are excellent but grays and light greens are almost equally good. Another suggestion is the use of "cold water" paint. This can be renewed each year and is especially adapted to this room because it has all the drying, cleansing advantages of the familiar whitewash.

If the floor is of cement by all means paint it with a special **cement floor paint,** tile red in color. It will take at least two coats and three are better. In painting use this same red paint for one foot up on the walls. A laundry floor must be washed and the darkened baseboards and wall space yield a much better appearance than the lighter wall paint would give. Do not try to use either floor wax or oil polishes on this floor, instead use a mop and an occasional hose treatment allowing the excess water to run down the open floor drain, which should be in every laundry.

Door and window trim where one can select the ideal should **be** plain and unpaneled, but these so-called slab doors, while made in stock sizes, are more expensive and few of us feel that we can put them in this room. However, there is a real

EQUIPMENT, CHOICE AND INSTALLATION

saving of time and care possible when they are installed, so they are worth consideration at least. Either a **hard waterproof varnish** treatment for the woodwork or a plain **oil** treatment on the natural wood will be found acceptable for the laundry. I would not advise paint, either light or dark.

Ventilation is most important; moreover, it should be secured without placing the ironing equipment in so direct a draft that it will cool the ironing machine shoe. For this reason **transoms** are the ideal provision. In case these are impossible see that your windows are screened the entire surface, then open laundry windows from the top and you will obtain almost equally good results.

Wiring for the laundry should take into consideration **two** things, illumination and sufficient provision for service outlets. Be sure that the wiring circuits upon which these appliances are installed are not overloaded. If this has not been done you will be troubled by blown fuses and the washing must come to a standstill until new fuses are inserted. The best remedy is to be sure that the laundry appliances are wired on a separate circuit. Again, use separable plugs and never connect into a lighting fixture. It is especially easy with a heavy washing machine or a hand iron to tear out the fixture, short circuit it or both. Therefore, install a sufficient number of baseboard or wall outlets to serve your various equipment.

For **lighting** there is nothing better than an overhead indirect fixture of sufficient power to light the entire room.

BUSINESS OF HOUSEKEEPING

But if your laundry has the small sewing table an added desk lamp here, might be an advantage.

Actual **equipment** of your laundry can be as simple or elaborate as your purse allows. The bare essentials are the **washing machine** and the **ironing machine.** Either one alone is lonesome for its twin. I also like to include some form of **drying machine.** Indeed more housekeepers would I feel assume the actual laundry work in their homes with machine equipment if they but realized that satisfactory drying could be accomplished in the house during inclement days.

In addition to the older type of **laundry-stove-heated dryers** there are today a number of satisfactory compact **gas heated machines** and for localities not served by this fuel there is a well-made small but powerful **electric centrifugal dryer** that whirls the clothes ready for the ironing machine in a few moments. While nothing can take the place of sun and air as routine practice in drying, nevertheless one of these dryers is a distinct advantage for emergency use. In many localities such a dryer will find a use during at least six months of the year.

Where gas is available an **ironing machine** is in my opinion as important as the washing machine. Indeed it acts as almost more of a time saver. For instance, many housekeepers are able to obtain their laundry washed for a reasonable figure and with reasonably good results. Delivered rough dry, they can sprinkle and accomplish the ironing

EQUIPMENT, CHOICE AND INSTALLATION

on an ironing machine at a real saving in laundry figures. The present model **open-end ironer** is capable of performing at least three quarters of the entire ironing and at a saving of one-half to three-quarters of the time. I am quite aware that these figures are impressively high but they are not the result of a single housekeeper's experience; indeed over a hundred housekeepers reported to Good Housekeeping Institute that this range had been their experience. In this connection I am also including an ironing time study covering the hand and machine method as used by one of these housekeepers.

IRONING TIME STUDY

Ironed by hand with electric iron—time, 2 hours and 5 minutes.

3 girl's fancy dresses	1 Tuxedo collar
2 baby dresses, ruffled	2 cuffs
1 baby bib	4 men's soft shirts
1 woman's gingham dress	4 boy's blouses
1 vestee	1 boy's Norfolk coat
1 boy's trousers	

21 pieces

Ironed by machine—time, 1 hour and 25 minutes.

1 large bedspread	8 men's handkerchiefs
4 large sheets	1 boy's belt (white pique)
10 crib sheets	1 man's linen trousers (ironed to crotch, top by hand)
5 pillow cases	3 boy's khaki trousers
2 baby pillow cases	5 child's dresses
4 hand towels	1 child's pinafore
5 tea towels	2 pair panties
1 roller towel	4 pair bloomers
2 small tablecloths	5 baby dresses
5 napkins	1 kimono baby slip
1 round centerpiece	1 Gertrude petticoat
3 round doilies	3 kitchen aprons
3 linen bibs	8 women's handkerchiefs
9 soft collars	

98 pieces

Ironing Boards

Possibly the **ironing board** is the next consideration. Use a sturdy rigid one to insure steadiness. Look for this especially in the board of the folding type. The height of the board is important because one that is too low makes the labor of ironing even harder. At the same time it has been my experience that many working laundresses use and like a lower board, probably because they have developed stronger back muscles than the average housekeeper and do not mind expending real muscle strength. But for the woman who irons only weekly or semi-weekly an ironing surface thirty-four inches from the floor is a convenient height. For the taller woman 36 inches may be better. But these dimensions are suggestive only. Try and work out a height that is most convenient for you. Before covering the **board** pad it well with wool felt or use a discarded quilted silence cloth. Old blankets are excellent, but whatever is used, be sure that there is enough of it to really pad to a cushiony depth. Never use a seamed pad. For the outside new unbleached muslin or a discarded sheet makes an excellent cover. It, too, should be free from seams and wrinkles. In putting it on, pull it just as taut as you can and fasten it securely, using either a generous number of strong safety pins, horseblanket size; the especially designed pins for ironing board use; or strong tapes attached to the cover every four or five inches. Finally keep two covers and interchange their use.

EQUIPMENT, CHOICE AND INSTALLATION

Electric Irons

You will need one or two **hand irons** depending upon the amount of work to be done. The six pound weight is the best selection for general use but a smaller four pound iron proves an excellent auxiliary. Be sure that a wall plate outlet is provided so that the ironer can forget the cord. This plate should preferably be about one foot above the ironing board and set close to the edge nearest the worker. When set as usual, centered in the board, there is a necessity for dragging the iron cord across the ironing board, which my suggestion obviates. A remarkable convenience in **electric irons** is the inserted switch. It obviates the constant removal of the plug and appreciably lengthens the life of the iron. To take out and put in a plug often means an inconvenience that prevents the user doing it unless she is directly interested in the electric bill, or in saving for her employer the maximum amount of current. Learn to disconnect at the iron or at the insert rather than at the socket, if a lamp socket has to be used. Don't *leave* an iron to heat. "Stay by the ship" for the short time required. Iron all heavy materials with the current on throughout the process, but for lighter fabrics learn to turn the current off, and iron by retained heat. If your electric rate costs 10¢ a kilowatt hour the iron will cost between five and six cents to operate each hour provided the current is in use all that time.

The Laundry Trays

Laundry trays may be one or two in number with the **washing machine** installed beside or in front of one of them. These trays should be set 36 inches from the rim to the floor. Use a platform to raise a washing machine to this level if it should be necessary. Some perfectly good machines are not quite high enough for this setting; which has been proven by years of test experience as most convenient for the work. Instead of the usual tray if you are planning new installations I suggest the so-called "slop sink." It is straight-sided and has in consequence a greater capacity for its size. Moreover, the sloping tray is not needed unless hand rubbing on a board is to be done. A still further suggestion: set one of the tubs 40 inches to the roll rim instead of 36. Such a tray is most excellent for hand washing of fine work as laces, silks, small wools, and the baby's daily wash. The squeezing motion entailed in this kind of hand washing can then be accomplished with ease and a straight back. Moreover, there is a decided advantage in getting this type of wash out of the bathroom, at present a popular place for this fine laundering.

In making your **washing machine** selection I have only two suggestions. First, choose one that is sold and therefore serviced in your neighborhood, in preference to one that is unfamiliar. In this way you will be assured of a maximum of dealer interest and service when "garage work" on your machine may be necessary.

EQUIPMENT, CHOICE AND INSTALLATION

Second, protect yourself from poorly made and designed machines by selecting only such machines as have been approved by Good Housekeeping Institute. Any principle of operation, cylinder, vacuum cup, oscillating, or a variation or combination of them, will give satisfactory washing results. It is preëminently a question of skilful design and good construction on the part of the manufacturer. Let your own preference as to the type of machine you prefer guide you.

But there is no exception to the necessity of **piping** the washing machine to both hot and cold water, and with a **mixing faucet** if possible. Again, connect it with the waste pipes or provide a floor drain for those machines that are not adapted to a rigid plumbing connection. You can pipe a cylinder type machine and certain of the vacuum cup type, but the oscillating type and the vacuum cup type with the centrifugal dryer are not well adapted to plumbing connection. If the **floor drain,** however, is properly placed the emptying is as easy if not easier than with the rigid connection. In the latter case an occasional inspection must be made to prevent clogging with lint, etc. If the plumber installs the machine with an extra trap provision it is a great convenience in caring for this.

I know of nothing more important than proper water connection; do not expect the laundress to exchange her **piped laundry tubs** for a machine to which she must carry water, and then must empty! In few cases will she be enthusiastic over the exchange. Carrying water is hard work, and I think it has been responsible for much lack of appreciation of the washing machines.

A sewing table stocked with mending materials is somewhat of an innovation in the home laundry; but it is found in commercial laundries and I know you will find it feasible and a time saver to accomplish certain mending as buttons, etc., while the clothes are rough dry. An occasional bit of fine mending is even needed before washing.

Where a **kitchen cabinet** is not provided shelves can be built into the laundry to accommodate utensils and supplies. The main point is to see that laundry utensils are kept for laundry use and are never exchanged with those used in the kitchen.

Occasionally certain clothes will require **boiling**, therefore, **a copper boiler** and a **stick** for stirring must be provided. If the fuel is gas, select a low laundry stove design, not more than 26 inches from the floor—or buy a two or three burner plate and set it on a metal covered table cut down so that the overall height will be 26 inches.

Finally, every stage of the handling of the clothes is immeasurably helped by the **work bench** put on casters. I had a carpenter make mine with an area that just accommodates the clothes basket, and a height of only 16 inches. A push of the foot carries the basket the length of the room if necessary and all stooping to your task is forever elimi-

EQUIPMENT, CHOICE AND INSTALLATION

nated. In this connection I want to say that setting up exercises even for the soldiers are not kept up throughout a period as long as the average washday; which is sufficient answer to certain enthusiastic advocates of "old-fashioned housework for health's sake."

I am often asked if it is possible to train helpers to use machinery and to care for it properly. In my experience every bit of machinery that was properly installed to really save labor has been enthusiastically accepted after a trial. Provided the housekeeper herself knows how to use the machines she can easily teach a maid how to use them. It is well worth the time and effort to stay by with the demonstrator of the machine you purchase so that you, yourself, will know just how to oil it and just how to use it. **Repair charges** on machinery for the household are deserving of a word. It is no more true of household appliances than it is of automobiles that they will never need repairs and renewal. I am afraid that we as women have been taught to expect too much of such machines. "Garage" charges for our machines are perfectly fair and to be expected when there has been reasonable wear obtained from them. An occasional renewal of parts as they become worn out is to be expected. Careful oiling and the same care given to household machines that is accorded the family automobile will mean that all of the larger equipment may last an entire lifetime of service with such renewal of parts. The length of service yielded by a well-made machine is entirely a question of use and care.

If you have two or three motors in service I have found it to pay to have a fixed **monthly inspection** by an electrician. This has prevented all emergency visits at a cost of two and sometimes three workers' time, and in the end proves the least expensive method of caring for them, unless you can do it yourself.

Chemical Reagents for the Laundry

The **chemicals** needed in the laundry require more than a mere mention. On the shelves should be kept the following supplies, renewed as they become used up in the various processes:

Enameled or nickeled starch kettle
Coarse strainer
Fine strainer for starch
Enameled preserving kettle for boiling small things as handkerchiefs, etc., or for use in dyeing stockings, etc.
Two clothes baskets, medium sized.
Three smaller baskets for handling the small washes as baby's, silk, etc.
Clotheslines, pins and bag.
Clothesprops and clothestick for boiling
Glass measuring cup and glass dropper
Bottle sprinkling device
Wood or enameled mixing spoons
Strong sharp knife or grater for shaving soap
Funnel
Dusters
Flannel and cheesecloth

EQUIPMENT, CHOICE AND INSTALLATION

Heavy paper
Extra ironing cover
Pins
Cloth covers for each machine while not in use; discarded bedspreads of the dimity type have proved excellent
In addition the reagent shelf should be stocked with:
  Liberal number of jars of melted soap
  Soap flakes and powdered soaps
  Water softeners in the form of package borax and washing soda solution
  Wax for irons
  Alum and salt for setting colors
  Javelle water for stains
  Starch
  Gum arabic for organdies
  Bluing, lingerie tints and dyes

AN IRONING BOARD SUGGESTION

I have found it extremely helpful to pad both sides of my ironing board, and then make a bag of muslin which fits the board snugly. A few tacks at the wide end of the board hold the cover in place. One side is clearly marked, and the members of the family know they must use this side for pressing trousers, serge skirts, or anything liable to stain or soil the cover. This leaves the other side always clean and ready for the regular laundry work.

—Good Housekeeping Discovery.

A NEW USE FOR THE SOAP SHAKER

A soap shaker will be found invaluable when re-dipping fabrics with soap dye. Place the cake of soap dye in the soap shaker and shake it back and forth in the water as when using soap. In this way the hands are not stained, and an even distribution of color is insured.

—Good Housekeeping Discovery.

COAT HANGERS FOR DRYING CLOTHES

When compelled to dry clothes in the house on account of bad weather, I use coat hangers for each garment and hang them on the line. This plan utilizes space to a wonderful extent and is very satisfactory. The coat hangers can be purchased for five cents each and frequently, two for five cents. *—Good Housekeeping Discovery.*

CHAPTER III

Washing Formulas

SOAPS AND SOAP COMPOUNDS

SUCCESSFUL washing by machine is not dependent upon any one variety of **soap**. I have never used one that could not be handled with perfectly satisfactory results.

But successful washing is extremely dependent upon the form and manner in which this soap is used. Indeed it is safe to say that if you have not already used your chosen soap in a dissolved form, you have not attained the utmost efficiency of which the machine is capable.

There are **plain laundry soaps** and **borax laundry soaps**, **naphtha** soaps and various other special soaps; sometimes in combinations with bluing. All are good, but don't try to use them in either bar or chip form or cut into even the smallest pieces. Instead dissolve them by **shaving or grating** first; then, with all save the naphtha soaps, use hot water and heat until the soap is dissolved. Use one-half pound of **soap chips** or a **bar of soap** to two quarts of water.

Naphtha soap has an additional solvent in the form of naphtha and it must be protected against evaporation. Therefore, in the case of naphtha soap shave a bar into each of two quart jars, fill them with lukewarm water, cover and place on the shelf for use.

There is a decided advantage in making up these formulas each washday for use the next week. In this way the shelves are assured to be never empty. I have known of more than one poor wash to result from the laundress lacking the soap solution and in too great a haste to get the wash out on the line to first make solutions. Such haste never pays.

Flake and powdered soaps do not need this preliminary dissolving, and if it were not for their greater cost, their convenience of use would undoubtedly insure their routine place in the home laundry. Even so it is well to keep a supply on hand for any emergency failure of the solution. My only suggestion is: to keep the soap flakes a bit "under your thumb" or you will find the "emergency" arising often.

Softeners

In connection with **soap in solution** there is an equally important phase of its use. Just why the time at which the suds is developed should have any influence on the actual washing efficiency, frankly, I do not know. But repeated trials have amply demonstrated that the water,

WASHING FORMULAS

and softener if used, and the soap solution should be agitated into suds *before any clothes are put into the machine*. Try two batches in the two ways and I am sure you will find, as I do, that when the soiled clothes are put in, then the water added, and finally the soap, there is very little suds developed even with a great deal of soap used, and the cleansing power seems to be seriously lessened. If you run the machine empty of clothes but containing the water, softener if used, and soap solution for two or three moments you will see for yourself the rich suds that are produced: sufficient promise of the efficient wash they will insure.

In addition to the **soap solution** many housekeepers will need **water softeners** because there are few waters available that are really "soft." **Rain water** is the nearest to this condition and the old-fashioned housekeeper had a real reason for storing rain water in hogsheads for her laundry use; she well knew that washing was a simplified process when water was soft. **Borax** will dissolve quickly and may be added to the water in powdered form, if done before the clothes are put in the machine. If water conditions permit it, the borax in combination with soap may be used. Again, **washing soda** is entirely harmless to the clothes if properly used in the form of solution. Make this solution by pouring one gallon of hot water over one pound of washing soda. One-half cup of this strength solution is a good unit for the machine tub.

Always add it after the water has been placed in the tub and before either soap or clothes are put in. The amount you will need is absolutely dependent upon your own water conditions as well as upon the character of the soiled linen. It is safe to say that more will be needed when water is very hard and it is further safe to say that more will be needed when there are any marked odors of perspiration, or excretions incidental to certain chronic illnesses.

Remember you are using it as a soap saver to counteract some of the hardness in the water; therefore, take utmost advantage of the chemical reaction between water salts and the soda. It leaves a more or less softened water for the soap solution to develop into suds.

And this indeed brings us to the discussion of one of the biggest problems of the home laundry: numbers of housekeepers are trying to make their clothes clean in a water so hard and brackish as to be impossible of "**suds.**" Unquestionably then the character of your water supply should somewhat affect the choice of soap and washing formula. In the majority of water conditions, good results can be obtained with any of them. But where there is trouble it usually develops as a sticky deposit almost like tiny specks of gray chewing gum appearing on the clothes. It is extremely difficult to remove, and ironing makes it practically indelible.

In these cases I suggest that too much water softener has been used in the form of soda or borax either in solution

WASHING FORMULAS

or in combination with soap. It is a better washing principle I believe in such cases to attempt no water softening at all; instead choose your soap carefully and count on using just about double the quantity.

Naphtha soap works especially well under such circumstances. It was my experience to be forced to use a particularly hard water during one summer. I used naphtha soap made into solution as directed. Four bars each week accomplished perfectly the laundry that involved linen for five beds, as well as the balance of a family wash of this size. Try it if you are thus troubled and I am sure that you will be convinced of its efficiency.

There may even be conditions of **water hardness** so excessive that they warrant the installation of one of the small **water softening plants,** especially designed for the household. These are practical, not unduly expensive, and of course completely correct this evil. Their cost of installation and maintenance is directly dependent upon the degree of hardness of the water to be corrected.

Washing formulas may then consist of any one of the following four: Neutral soap in solution accompanied by a water softener, either in the form of borax or washing soda in solution. Second, a solution of plain laundry soap which is the manufacturer's own mixture of soap and softener. Third, naphtha soap in solution. Fourth, a combination of soap, bluing and softener, to be found in flake and bar form. Select the one you prefer and use as stipulated; as a solution and as a rich suds which cleanses the fabric by a combined mechanical and chemical process.

BLUES AND TINTS

There is so wide a difference in behavior among **bluings** that many washing defects can be traced to their incorrect use. There are three kinds that lend themselves well to modern home laundry use. Possibly **Prussian blue** is most commonly used. It is a bright greenish blue in color and almost invariably sold in liquid form. Housekeepers have liked it because of its color and the ease with which it is used. But it has a real drawback in the fact that it contains a salt of iron which may turn to iron rust, in the presence of alkali and particularly when heat is applied, as in ironing. You will see, then, the necessity for an absolutely thorough rinsing. If a trace of soap is left in the fabric through careless rinsing it will combine with the bluing and the result is a discoloration due to iron oxide. You can readily see, therefore, that Prussian blue entails exceptional care in rinsing. If you are not sure the bluing you are using is Prussian, test it by heating a little with a strong solution of washing soda. It will turn a yellowish red and the red iron rust will deposit in the bottom of the utensil.

Ultramarine is another bluing entirely different both in composition and in behavior. It used to be the blue lapis lazuli stone finely ground but today it is more often prepared in the chemical laboratory and carries with it a large amount of clay filler. It is, of course, insoluble and yields a tint to the clothes by depositing its fine grains evenly on the threads of the fabric. The finer the grain the more even will be the bluing result. It is usually sold in ball or block form. And in its use there are two points to note: Always tie it in a small cloth and dip and squeeze the water until the desired strength is secured. Test out the bluing water with a white cloth to see if it is the right color. Second, such a bluing must be used with the water kept constantly in motion to prevent the particles settling unevenly on the clothes or at the bottom of the tub. Shake the clothes out well and attempt only a few pieces at a time.

The bluing color yielded by ultramarine is very good. You can tell if your bluing is ultramarine by letting it stand in a glass when the blue powder will settle to the bottom.

Aniline bluing is a new form to many housekeepers, although it is popular with the commercial laundries. It is found in powdered or crystal form and is, therefore, a soluble bluing with no waste. Like the ultramarine it can produce no iron rust stain. It must usually be bought from laundry supply houses, either by the ounce or the pound. It is so strong a dye that a much smaller quantity is required than of any other blue on the market. Its color is good and it adapts itself to a variety of tints from pale blue to almost purple. Indeed it is the difficulty the inexperienced find in getting the same tint each time that has prevented this bluing becoming more popular. With this bluing it is just as essential that all soap is carefully rinsed out of the clothes because it does not set well in the presence of alkalies. Again, it is a powerful dye and if too much is used it is difficult to wash and bleach it out.

You will see that the disadvantages of each one of these bluings are readily counteracted by correct using, and it becomes then a most satisfactory plan to select the brand which seems best suited to your individual needs and then accustom yourself to its individual use. The accurate measurement of bluing is a new thought to the experienced laundress but it is worth a trial if aniline is used. It must be remembered also that the effect of bluing is different on different weaves. Open weaves as toweling take bluing so readily that a weaker solution is required than for the most closely woven sheeting, etc. Learn to know the possibilities and guard against the defects of the bluing you select.

Lingerie Tints and Dyes

But bluing is after all but one of the tints used in the laundry of today. **Soap tints** in the form of cakes or flakes or as a rinsing powder insure the original color throughout the life of the garment. Flesh, orchid, peach, maize, blue and the new shade of green are the most

WASHING FORMULAS

popular. A supply of each one of these may be on the reagent shelf.

When making the soap tints, a satisfactory method is to make the solution first, and add it to the water. Again, it is a real dye saver to have the first washing of the garments accomplished with regular soap, jelly or flakes.

Another method of extending the **dye soap** is to add enough more **white soap flakes** or **jelly** to insure the added cleansing suds. Most of the soap flakes dissolve rapidly enough if very hot water is poured over them, adding cold water as soon as the soap is dissolved to yield the right washing temperature.

If the tint you are using is in the form of a cake you have a choice of procedure. Either make it into a soap jelly by shaving it and dissolving it in one-half cupful of hot water or put the cake in a soap shaker, and shake in very hot water until you have obtained a sufficiently strong suds.

The amount to be used depends absolutely on the amount of fabric and the depth of color you wish. In general use the package directions.

Tinting with a powder to be used in the rinse is perhaps the simplest of the methods and is, of course, merely an exchange of a tint for the bluing. Be as careful in washing and rinsing as if bluing were used. In preparing the powder, pour hot water directly on it and cool down to lukewarm temperature. Unless you have a special reason for changing the proportion, one teaspoonful to each gallon of water will make a satisfactory color rinse.

STARCHES AND STARCHING

The days of prodigal use of **starch** have gone by with the fashion of "rustling" silks. The aim today is to replace only the manufacturer's dressing which yielded the fine sheen and newness to the fabric. Instead of being stiff, it must have its original firmness but keep its pliability with the gloss and finish that tends to repel moisture and soil.

Many mothers discovered to their sorrow that the unstarched, unironed fabrics advocated for children's clothes made so much more washing that the labor-saving quality was problematical. This was because the roughened fabric attracted dirt and smooching instead of repelling it, as the smoothly starched and ironed fabric does. For this reason use starch with discretion, but don't discard it entirely from your laundry régime.

Few of us realize that there is a variety in starches adapted for laundry work as: corn, wheat, rice and blended starches. The blended starches are combinations of two or all of the others, with possibly some borax and paraffine or wax included. This is what the purchaser usually gets when she buys a packaged form of "laundry starch." The quality of starch which makes it adapted to laundry

WASHING FORMULAS

dressing is its stickiness or tenacity, called by the chemist viscosity. Wheat starch has less of this viscosity but more pliability and rice has the least of all.

The secret of having **starch free from lumps** is to first mix the starch with a small amount of cold water. Stir it constantly as you pour it into the correct amount of water that is boiling. This boiling temperature bursts open the starch grains, producing an evenly stiffened mass. Boil five minutes to completely cook the starch. A thick starch for heavy cottons uses one gallon of water and three fourths cups of cornstarch, or one and a quarter cups of either rice or wheat starch. A medium starch for lingerie is made by using one-half the amount of starch and the same quantity of water. Reduce this strength one-half by adding hot water and it is excellent for voile waists and similar very thin cotton fabrics. Such a starch thickness is not enough to add an appreciable stiffening to the fabric, but does afford a smoothness to the ironed garment that repels soil. Keep the starch hot and covered until ready for use. If it cools to produce the heavy film on top, strain it before use.

An easy procedure in starching is to add the starch to the laundry tray and starch those garments that need this original strength first, and those that require the least strength last. Run the clothes through the wringer, loosening the tension. This protects the hands, for it is not comfortable to wring clothes from starch as hot as it should be used. And it further helps to distribute the starch evenly through the fabric.

Just a suggestion for both **bluing and starching** in machines having a centrifugal dryer. In this case use a much weaker solution of both bluing and starch. You may have to experiment a little to determine the best strength for your work, but it is a safe suggestion to start with fifty per cent. reduction in solution.

By the way, the manufacturer has ample reason for his blending, because he thus takes advantage of the various properties of the starches themselves and the borax, alum and paraffine, although not absolutely necessary, unquestionably improve the starch, making it both easier to use and more uniform in results.

Gum arabic and dextrine are starch substitutes especially adapted for the very delicate fabrics as organdie and baby's nainsook. The proportion of two tablespoonfuls to a quart of water will give these fabrics an appearance and body much like the original. In purchasing dextrine be sure that you get white dextrine for white or light colors. In preparing either the dextrine or gum arabic, they need only be dissolved in hot water.

WASHING FORMULAS

WHEN STARCHING CLOTHES

In doing the washing for my family in our electric washing-machine, I found that the starching of from forty to sixty garments and pieces of household linen was the most tedious and disagreeable part of the whole undertaking. Almost immediately I happened upon this plan which has proved a real time-saver. I make about three-quarters of a gallon of starch. When all the washing is finished and the clothes have been rinsed and wrung dry, I put about half of the pieces to be starched, shaken out lightly, into one of the stationary tubs. I pour half of the hot starch over them and wring them one by one through the power wringer, the top ones first. As the starch drips off the wringer board, I hold the next piece under to catch it, occasionally sopping the starch out of the corners of the tub also, and then repeating the operation till all the clothes are wrung through. Then I put the rest of the pieces in the tub and pour the balance of the starch over them, repeating the wringing process. The starch is evenly distributed through the clothes, and I have no trouble with lumps when ironing them. If any piece is desired very stiff, it can be dipped in the starch first. —*Good Housekeeping Discovery.*

CHAPTER IV

Laundry Methods

The Chemistry of Washing

IT was a manufacturer who asked me somewhat skeptically, I will admit, where I learned to wash. The kernel of truth as to the mechanics of washing came to me in the Village of Waquoit, a part of Falmouth Township on Cape Cod. My childhood summers were passed there, also the summers of a family of six boys, who were dubbed "the white duck brigade." Now these boys had to do their own washing and they were always immaculate. Here was their method: Each morning as they went out in their catboat, just as soon as the eel grass zone was passed, they threw overboard the "white ducks" tied to a line. Until the sail was over, their suits cut through the water, only to be pulled on board upon arrival at the mooring, wrung dry, and stretched flat on the decks beneath weights.

Here in a nutshell is the mechanical principle of washing. Send a cleansing fluid through fabric with sufficient force to dislodge dirt.

LAUNDRY METHODS

But the chemistry of washing was harder to get. It required long years of puzzling over wrist-band and neck-band soils that are not easily removed. It required the watching of laundress after laundress, one a good laundress who washed easily, one a poor laundress who washed with great muscular effort, but grimy clothes. It required close study in a bacteriological laboratory to trace the question of sanitation and germ growth. It required practical washing experience.

Out of all of this has grown a few simple principles, which will make more intelligible and helpful any washing directions that you may have been using.

First, in spite of any directions to the contrary that may accompany your washing machine, **do not use boiling water or very hot water** in which to wash your clothes. And here is the reason. Test factory washes were naturally composed of garments that were easy to obtain, like the men's overalls and working jumpers, and the towels that were stained with machine oils and greases. In every case you will note that the soil was held in the fabric by a vegetable or mineral oil. These oils unite very readily with hot water and soap to form emulsions and saponifications, and in forming either of these the dirt that is held in the fabric is loosened. Hence, the hotter the water the quicker and cleaner was the washing. I am convinced after conferences with numerous manufacturers, that here lies the source of many incorrect directions for using a washing machine.

The soils met with in a family wash are radically different, and far more difficult to remove. I have mentally analyzed them to contain the following materials and will try to tell you the properties of these materials as they affect washing. The kind that we are most familiar with is the black soil or dirt that is always held in the fabric by another more or less sticky compound. In the case of the **overalls** it was a vegetable or mineral oil, but in the case of **wearing apparel** it is animal fat. It is the animal fats that make the most trouble when boiling water is used, because each globule of them is encased in a film of albuminous material and it is cooked into the fabric by boiling water instead of being loosened to release the grime. Now this is the secret of much of your trouble with **wristbands and neckbands**. It explains why you have to rub after washing in your machine. It explains the yellowish stain on **pillow cases** after repeated machine washing in hot water. In the same way **fruit, coffee and tea stains** which have dried are hopelessly set by soaking or washing in too hot water, although these stains yield to actually boiling water when applied directly to the fresh stain. Had you used lukewarm water you would have taken advantage of both the mechanics and the chemistry of washing.

The old-fashioned method of hand washing safeguarded you against using too hot water, because you could not put your hands into it. Wristbands and neckbands responded easily to the laundress who was clever enough

LAUNDRY METHODS

not to rub her knuckles but to "souse" suds through the fabric. Are there not, then, good practical reasons—based upon the science of chemistry to be sure, but none the less practical for that—for my insistence upon your use of lukewarm to medium hot water?

The second point that I insist upon is that **soap should be in solution,** and this, too, has a chemical reason. Solution in its actual definition merely means the distribution of the particles so evenly that one spoonful contains as much as another spoonful. Is there not then good reason for having your washing solution of this even strength?

The third thing I insist upon is that **you shall not soap the clothes,** and the reason for this is that you clog up the pores, making it difficult for the rush of suds to pass through them and making it doubly difficult to rinse out the soap which is absolutely necessary to whiteness of the clothes.

The fourth thing I insist upon is that you **shall not soak the clothes,** the reason for this being that you weaken the washing solution, because the clothes instead of being dry and light are heavy with dirty water that dilutes the washing fluid.

Fifth, work out your own choice of soap and softener, and use it according to directions given on page 148. Increase the soap strength of your suds in direct proportion to the amount of work you expect it to do. For instance, a solution that would be amply strong to care for **table linen and**

bed linen might not be strong enough by one-half for **underwear and body linen** in general. **Children's rompers and white stockings** offer a real problem. The latter are so close in texture that it is difficult to force the washing fluid through the fabric with sufficient force to completely cleanse. Make the proportion, then, an individual problem to be worked out by you since you are the only one who can know the conditions in which the clothes are used.

In certain sections of the country there is a clay so sticky as to present a problem all its own. We can only urge that the principle of washing outlined for you is the right one, properly controlled to suit your condition.

Perhaps the sixth point is the most important hint for the mother of small children. The handling of a large quantity is no longer the biggest work item when washing by machine, as it was when washing by hand. Therefore, increase generously the number of pieces allowed the children. Do not let them wear **socks and rompers** long enough to need harsh methods. Wash more and oftener but less soiled pieces. Forget the old hand washing point of view, for the new machine washing is easier work.

Boiling should be optional. There will always be certain clothes that require boiling, as **handkerchiefs, personal napkins,** etc. There may even be periods of illness where boiling the **bedding** is important to accomplish. But routine boiling of the **household linen** is not necessary provided sufficient hot—scalding hot—rinses are used. The

LAUNDRY METHODS

hotter the water, the nearer it approaches the steam scald of the commercial laundry, the whiter will be the clothes. If any particular garment or group bothers you, take particular pains to wash it in fresh washing solution and rinse it two or three times in hot water before you put it into the cold rinse. Indeed so important is the rinsing to proper washing of clothes that it is not too much to say that the most perfect results are just in proportion to the hotness and abundance of the rinse waters.

We urge the **rinsing** in the machine because it is most efficiently done there; indeed no amount of hand rinsing quite takes the place of the powerful agitation produced by the machine. You are not taking fullest advantage of your machine if you attempt to do the hot rinse by hand.

A conservative housekeeper may ask how clothes can be kept **sanitary without boiling.** Do you realize that the temperature of the iron or ironer with which the clothes are ironed is from 500° F. down to 350° F.? Is not this fully as efficient as boiling or 212° F. in destroying germs? If clothes are not ironed there might be an argument for boiling for sanitation, as a routine practice.

Routine of the Family Wash

In making ready for washday be sure that **machines** are oiled, clean and ready for use. Glance at **soap solutions**

and supplies and be assured that they are available for the use of the laundress.

Next **sort the linen** into its usual divisions—table linen, bed linen, body linen, colored clothes, silks and wool, hose and the general scrub and dust cloths from the household cleaning closets. Discard any that need special stain treatment.

Into the **washing machine** run a supply of boiling hot water. Add water softener if you use it and soap solution, then run in cooler water to yield the correct temperature. It should not be hotter than the hand can bear. Connect the machine, turn on the motor switch, then the machine clutch and run the machine two or three minutes to develop suds. Open and add your first batch of clothes, dry from the sorting table. This tubful consists of table linen and the machine can be more nearly overloaded with this wash than any other group, because it is presumably the least soiled. Even so it is well to mix the sizes. Don't include in one run three or four large tablecloths even though the capacity of the machine is rated at six sheets. Much better washing results are obtained with a mixture of sizes. Two tablecloths with their napkins, doilies and small lunch cloths are a much better grouping.

In any case wash for fifteen or twenty minutes, depending on the amount of soil. At this time it is possible to work in an occasional bit of stain removal that will make it pos-

LAUNDRY METHODS

sible to include the stained cloth or table napkin in the next run of clothes.

At the end of the washing period, **wring the clothes** as dry as possible into a **waiting tub.** I accent this dry wringing because the more completely the washing solution is removed from the fabric, the easier will be the rinsing process. The first wringing then must be as complete as possible.

At this point it is not necessary to discard the washing solution, instead add more soap solution, work the machine empty for a moment or two to develop fresh suds and add your second load of clothes: either a second batch of table linen or a first batch of bed linen. Again, with this group be sure that the sizes are varied, for the same reason as mentioned above. Again wring dry into the waiting tub.

At this point it may be necessary to empty out the entire solution and start fresh. Let your own conditions govern you here. Two runs and sometimes three may be made by means of additional soap solution. But you must be the judge of the exact point at which new solutions must be made. There is, of course, a real economy gained in soap to use it for as many runs as gives good results, but do not try to economize on the hot water of rinsing.

While the washing machine is taking care of the second batch of clothes it is, of course, possible to accomplish the rinsing in the tubs by hand, and it has been my experience that the experienced laundress will insist on doing it this way. To be sure, unless she can fill her time with stain removal or further sorting, she can show a real loss of time by waiting for the machine rinsing. It reads more efficient, I'll admit, but the rinsing results are so much less effective per time and per water and per gas used to heat the water that the housekeeper who once tries machine rinsing will, I feel, always continue it.

My plan then is to allow the **white clothes** to accumulate until the washing solution is to be changed for the first time. At this point instead of refilling the machine with a washing solution rinse out the soap solution with a little hot water and then fill with as hot water as you can obtain. Put in the clothes that have been wrung dry, a few at a time, and rinse for five minutes. Discard this rinsing solution often. I feel that this rinsing has such an influence upon the appearance of the clothes, that their whiteness is almost in proportion to the generosity of the water used at this point.

When they have been thus rinsed, wring as dry as possible into cold water. Let stand while you fill the machine with washing solution and start another run of clothes. From this time on the washing and rinsing processes dovetail into each other, since there is always something to be done.

From the **cold rinse,** wring the clothes into the blue rinse. This cold rinse, by the way, has a real blanching effect on the clothes and, therefore, should not be omitted, and clothes should be wrung as dry as possible. But in wringing from the bluing water wring loosely if the clothes are to be hung in the open. There is a real bleaching effect, resulting from the separation of the oxygen in the water, held in the clothes, through the action of the sun and air. This is the principle used in the famous "grass bleached" linen.

So soon as the white clothes are completed it is possible to make a machine washing of either the **silks or the wools** provided there are enough of either one to warrant it. In this case, however, use the mildest of **soap jelly or soap flakes.** Never use water softener for silks or wools. Wash as usual, wringing dry from the washing solution. Rinse according to the directions given for the special washing of silks and wools.

Wash the stockings separately and never mix cotton, silk or wool, since the three are so different in texture that it is not possible to keep any of them free from lint deposit unless they are separately handled.

Colored clothes need special handling. In general the solution should be the same as for flannel but it is wiser to wash but one colored frock at a time, unless one is perfectly certain of its fast color. I know of no calamity worse than the dyeing of a whole tubful of clothes through the "bleeding" of the dye in just one small romper. If but one is washed at a time until you are certain of its color, such a catastrophe will never occur. On the other hand there are certain **colored goods** that may be washed with the white clothes: as men's shirts and children's frocks and rompers of colored percale. Ginghams, chambrays and prints must be washed alone.

Finally in washing colored clothes be as careful in rinsing as with the white clothes. In general follow the same directions for the manipulation of the machine.

It is only fair to say for this whole method of washing that it is successful only when the suggestions are followed in their entirety. There have been sufficient responses from housekeepers who have used the method for it to have more than the assurance of one person's experience, but I have traced poor results to: failure to develop a good suds before attempting to wash; starting a load then stopping the machine long enough to attend to other duties while the clothes were left to stand in the washing solution; to the use of chunks of soap instead of dissolved soap; to occasionally mixing the various groups of linens; to the overcrowding of the machine and most often of all to careless and incomplete rinsing.

The Removal of Stains

Stains which you know will need more than just soap and water should be removed before washing. Do not expect to take out stains of any character from colored clothes without affecting the color. A bleach strong enough to remove a stain is strong enough to remove a dye.

LAUNDRY METHODS

Javelle water is a bleach for which you will have greatest use. You can purchase it at the drug store ready made, or you can make it yourself following this procedure: Put one pound of washing soda into an agate—never an aluminum—pan and add one quart of boiling water. Mix one-half pound of chloride of lime in two quarts of cold water. Let the mixture settle and pour the clear liquid into the dissolved soda. Bottle and keep in a dark place. To remove stains from white goods soak the article in equal quantities of Javelle water and hot water until the stain disappears, then rinse thoroughly in several waters and finally in diluted ammonia water. Javelle removes all stains and all colors and, therefore, should not be used on colored goods.

Oxalic acid may be prepared in the following manner: Dissolve one pound of crystals in three-fourths of a cupful of water.

Potassium Permanganate is made by dissolving two tablespoonfuls of permanganate crystals in one quart of water. Here are a few general rules you should keep in mind when using chemicals:

1. Apply chemical directly to the stain with a medicine dropper or glass stirring rod.

2. Do not allow the chemical to remain in contact with the material too long, as it will injure the fabric.

3. Rinse quickly and thoroughly after applying any chemical.

4. Chemicals will yellow silks and woolens and will remove color.

5. Heat accelerates chemical action.

6. If uncertain about the action of a reagent, test it first on a piece of material.

Common Stains and Their Reagents

Iron Rust—Apply lemon and salt and hold spot over steam.

Fruit—Hold stained portion taut over a bowl and pour boiling water on it from a height so that it will strike the fabric with force. For old stains, use Javelle water.

Coffee and Tea—Spread the stain over a bowl and cover the spot with a paste of borax and cold water. Then pour on it boiling water from a height. Stains of long standing will require Javelle water.

Chocolate—Apply a paste of borax and cold water, then pour boiling water from a height.

Grass—Wash a fresh stain in cold water without soap. Another method is to rub with molasses, let stand a few minutes and then wash out in warm water. The last resort is Javelle water.

Ink—Ink is most difficult of all stains because one must first identify the variety of ink. For that reason, the commercial eradicators, which may be purchased, we believe the best choice. Follow the directions on the box.

Mildew—This is a living plant which will not grow if light and air can reach the fabric. It may be removed while very fresh with cold water. In later stages apply potassium permanganate, then wash with warm water, use oxalic acid, and wash again. Oxalic acid will remove any brown left by the permanganate. Javelle water is a third method. If the mildew has attacked the fiber of the cloth, the strongest chemical will have no effect.

Vaseline—Wash a fresh stain with turpentine. The stain cannot be removed after it has been boiled.

Wagon grease—Rub the stain with lard, keeping a cloth beneath it. Then wash with warm water and soap.

Sprinkling and Folding

There is even a right and a wrong way to do these routine tasks. The supplies needed are a **sprinkling surface** that is absolutely clean and some method or device for distributing the water evenly. The experienced laundress scatters it with the hand over the fabric but few housekeepers can equal her skill. A whisk broom dipped into the water and snapped with the wrist above the fabric to be sprinkled proves effective. Or you can use one of the bottle sprinkling devices.

Hot water is more evenly distributed and by a form of "capillary attraction," so be sure that the temperature of the water is too hot to be borne by the hand if you are using one of these devices. If not, have it as hot as you can bear your hand. But after all sprinkling begins with the process of taking down from the line. If you will take the clothes down at the point that they are just "not dry" you will find it an ideal time to iron. Only practice will give you just the point that is best.

In general have clothes about twice as wet for the ironing machine as you do for ironing by hand. Again learn to keep a bowl of hot water handy to the ironing board; with a sponge or clean cloth you can dampen any portion of a garment that becomes dried or wrinkled during the ironing process.

Sheets should not need sprinkling, instead they should be removed from the line at the right point for ironing. If they do have to be sprinkled, fold lengthwise, then into quarters. Sprinkle one side, then the other, turn and sprinkle but one of the remaining quarters. Fold the unsprinkled quarter inside and roll into a compact hard bundle one-quarter the entire width of the sheet.

Towels are best sprinkled in an "every other one" layer. Sprinkle the first one generously, place a dry napkin on top, add another, and sprinkle this one generously. Continue sprinkling every other one in the bundle, then roll into a compact tight bundle. This rolling, by the way, has a real effect on the even distribution of water.

LAUNDRY METHODS

Pillow cases and napkins may be sprinkled in a similar way; in fact, all small flat work should be grouped together.

Garments should be sprinkled and rolled each in its **separate bundle**; otherwise they would dry before it is possible to complete the ironing.

Just a word about **mildew**. This is a mold growth that grows only under warm damp conditions. Clothes thrown wet down a laundry chute, as in the case of discarded towels, cause untold trouble during the warm months of the year. In large families it is not a bad practice to lock the clothes chute-door and use hampers for routine use. Each day this clothes hamper is emptied and the contents aired and dried before sending down the chute. This, of course, is not necessary where one worker takes care of the linen.

Even in sprinkling, this mildew problem deserves a word of caution, because it is possible for it to develop in the clothes basket when clothes are sprinkled and left unduly long before ironing. It should be possible to sprinkle a basket of clothes, cover with a dampened cloth, and have them perfectly ready for ironing the next morning. But, if weather conditions are very bad, it is inadvisable to dampen them more than two or three hours ahead of time. Remember in leaving them for the longer period they must be dampened more than for the shorter time. A **clothes basket or receptacle** that has once held badly mildewed clothes should be given a drastic scald and airing in the hot sun to kill any lurking mold growth, that may cause further trouble with new clothes.

Tub the Silks

Wash Silks are so common a fabric in the modern home that it has injected a new problem for washday. Silks do not soil easily probably because of the smoothness of the fiber. Moreover, soil is easily removed from the silk surface. And now that the manufacturer has solved the problem of producing a fabric that can be laundered to preserve its color and sheen, silk must be judged on its merits as a fabric in wear, convenience, comfort and cost. The following axioms touch the high spots of laundering silk:

1. Use only neutral soap.
2. Have the wash water lukewarm.
3. Have all rinse waters lukewarm.
4. Squeeze, not rub, out the soil.
5. Squeeze out the water—do not wring.
6. Hang the silks up to ''breathe'' in the air, but not the sun.
7. Roll separately.
8. Iron with only a medium-hot iron.

Just as in all washing, separate your **white and colored pieces.** Make a good, live suds first, by adding the soap to hot water, then cooling to lukewarm with cold water. Next put in your silks. Do not soak them, but wash at once, and use a squeezing rather than a rubbing motion to force the suds through the fiber.

LAUNDRY METHODS

Rinse at least twice in clear, warm water, the same temperature as that used for washing. Here lies one of the secrets of preserving the **whiteness of silks**. Extremes of temperature are disastrous, so do not subject the silk to either excessive heat or cold, but instead maintain a warm temperature for the whole procedure. Let me emphasize, too, thorough rinsing, for any suds left in the silk will surely yellow it when it is ironed.

The usual method of **wringing** should not be used. Instead, **squeeze the silk** between the hands, extracting as much water as possible, and at the same time putting no excessive strain on the delicate fibers. After squeezing as dry as possible, shake the silk and hang it up indoors for a very few minutes, fifteen to twenty. As an expert colored laundress aptly expressed it, "I hangs the silks up just long enough to let them breathe." The oxygen in the air has a bleaching effect on the fiber. Not only does this method tend to whiten the silk, but it also shortens the process greatly.

Before the silks are even partially dry, take them down and **roll** *each* individual piece separately in a towel. There are two methods of doing this rolling. One method is to roll the article itself and then wrap it well in a towel, and the second method is to spread the silk waist, or whatever it may be, on the towel and roll both together. The first method is the better if the silk has been allowed to "breathe," because most of the excess water will have evaporated, and if rolled up in this way, the article will be just moist enough for ironing. On the other hand, if the silk has not been hung up at all, the latter method is the better. The towel will absorb the excess water, leaving the moisture evenly distributed. A Turkish towel has greater absorbent qualities than any other type of towel, and so is more satisfactory for this purpose.

Then comes the **ironing**, and again temperature is most important. Hot irons will stiffen and crack the silk as well as yellow it, so be sure the iron is not too hot. Determine the right temperature through practice. Keep the silk rolled up until ready to iron, and then iron it thoroughly dry. If possible, iron the silk on the wrong side; it will tend to produce a newer appearance.

Plain colored silks can be kept uniform in tint with the colored soaps and tints. These **tints** come in flake, powder, and cake forms. The cake and flakes are soaps as well as tints and should be used in the wash water in addition to the plain suds. We have found it necessary to use plain soap also, because if enough of the soap tint is used to make a rich suds, the color will naturally be too dark. The powder is dissolved and used after the waist has been well rinsed. Put the powder in a white or very light bowl, and then pour over it a small amount of hot water and stir until it is in solution, then add cold water until the temperature is lukewarm and the desired shade has been reached. The degree of color will depend upon the amount

LAUNDRY METHODS

of tint used and the length of time the waist is left in the tint. Remember that the shade will be lighter after the waist is ironed than while it is wet.

Bluing should really be considered a tint. Unless you desire a bluish white, do not use it. Do not try to rescue an old waist by the use of bluing. The combination of the yellow and blue will give an undesirable greenish tint.

If you have many silk articles, especially underwear, you can wash them just as well, if not better, in your **washing machine,** taking the same precautions as when washing by hand. Wash for fifteen to twenty minutes—or longer, if necessary—in warm, "sudsy" water and rinse well in clear water of exactly the same temperature. The rest of the procedure is exactly the same as when washing by hand.

Wash very fine **Georgette crepes** separately, by hand. Although chiffons and Georgettes are not exactly delicate fabrics, they should be washed quickly and handled as little as possible.

Now then, you see there are only a few fundamental rules to follow when laundering silks, but they must be observed judiciously, or the results will be poor. If you will remember that silk, being an animal fiber, is easily affected by acid, alkali, and excessive heat, and treat it accordingly, following the method already outlined, I feel quite sure that the outcome will be entirely satisfactory. The life of the silk will be lengthened considerably, thus proving it an economical rather than an extravagant purchase.

BUSINESS OF HOUSEKEEPING

Rescue the Woolens

The family wardrobe contains so many sweaters, light wool scarfs, etc., that the washing of **small woolens** has become an item even when a baby's woolens do not have to be cared for.

Heretofore these have been the real bugbears of many housekeepers who dreaded to see the new fluffy garment become a hard, shrunken, misshapen one after the first laundering.

It is surprising, however, to what degree they respond to right treatment in laundering and it is not too much to expect that provided they are handled right a soft well-shaped sweater, baby's shirt, or blanket will be your reward.

Possibly a bit of knowledge as to what makes the **wool fiber** hard and shrunken together with plain directions how to wash will tend to overcome your reluctance to try these fabrics either by hand if they are small, or in the washing machine if they are too bulky for handling.

Each woolen thread unlike cotton has come from a living breathing animal whose coat is kept soft and woolly by an animal fat called **lanoline**. Now in the presence of an alkali this fat is undoubtedly extracted to a greater or less degree. And, because heat always aids any chemical action, hot water greatly increases the difficulty. The more you extract of this lanoline fat and the higher the temperature of the water, the harder and more shrunken will the wool fiber become.

I have washed blankets, pure wool flannel, sweaters and baby garments, and had them return to their original size and proportion, retaining their soft fluffiness by using the following method: First select a **neutral soap** or use any of the **prepared soap flakes,** or if you happen to have been interested in any special soap that is advocated for woolen use try it first on a square of pure wool flannel. Keep the original measurements and an unwashed sample. You will be enabled to detect any shrinking and difference in texture by a comparison. In any event dissolve the soap first and use as soap jelly.

To hot water add the **soap jelly** or **soap flakes,** then add cold water until lukewarm. Note this temperature either by feeling or a thermometer because every succeeding water that is used **must be of the same temperature.** Whip the lukewarm solution into strong suds; an easy way to do this for a small wash is with a hand-whip egg beater. Into the solution place one garment at a time or two pairs of socks or stockings. Wash by **squeezing** in the rich soap suds, using a motion beneath the suds similar to pulling candy. With each motion squeezing out the suds and then allowing more to penetrate the fiber. When clean gently pat out the excess suds; press gently but try to get as much out as possible, on the same principle as you use in the laundry when wringing dry as possible from the wash water.

Just here the procedure changes, depending upon the hardness of water which you must use. Never try to soften water with a water softener; but if the water supply is naturally soft, a much better result in soft texture will be obtained if you rinse in clear waters of the same temperature as the wash water. On the contrary, if your water supply is hard, it is often better to rinse with a small amount of soap jelly added to each rinse water much as you wash chamois gloves. By this soap rinsing in hard water, you are safeguarding against any possible loss of the wool fat. Of course, in proportion to the hardness of the water increase the amount of the soap jelly used in the rinse.

The next step in securing perfectly laundered wools is to overcome any tendency in **drying**, either to **stretch out of shape** or to **shrink out of shape**. An excellent method is to fasten a sheet or cloth taut over the clothes bars and then place the garment in exactly its original form. In the case of the sweater lay all the fullness in front, keeping the lines of the back accurate. Socks and stockings of wool should be stretched on frames; but this is not so expensive a procedure as it might seem, for excellent ones may be cut from cardboard. In using these **cardboard frames** I allow the stocking to become dry, or very nearly so before putting it on the frame. Then lay them away in the drawer and they stretch into perfect shape for wear. In cutting the cardboard frames use firm heavy cardboard, preferably the corrugated variety and pattern them after one of the wooden frames suitable in size. By this method there is no necessity for purchasing but the one wood frame. I have used this practice with baby's and children's wool stockings and socks and with adult's golf stockings, etc. In the case of the latter it is an excellent procedure to cut them off just below the cuff of the golf stockings so that there will be no danger of stretching that to the point of looseness.

Machine-Washed Blankets

Blanket washing should no longer be considered a bugaboo by the housekeeper. She need not look with distress at the pile of winter blankets which should have been washed last spring, or the summer blankets which must go away now. She need not resort to binding the blanket edges with cheese-cloth, or to any of the other methods of keeping blankets clean.

The **washing machine** has sufficiently lightened this task so that blankets may be washed more frequently in the home and need not be sent away to be cleaned. With this great boon to washing, it is quite possible to keep the blankets almost as sanitary as the sheets. As a labor saver, the machine cannot be excelled for washing heavy pieces like blankets, because it eliminates all that tiresome, back-bending strain. Furthermore, the machine is by far the

BUSINESS OF HOUSEKEEPING

best way to wash blankets, because of its power to force the suds through the fiber without any harsh rubbing, which is apt to be a temptation when washing by hand.

Blankets, whether all wool or partly wool, require the same care in washing as all other woolens. Keep the temperature for both washing and rinsing warm to medium hot, and use a **neutral soap** in either flake or jelly form, so that it will readily go into solution. Make the jelly yourself by softening one cake of soap in two quarts of water.

The first step in machine washing is to fill the tub up to the water line with water not above 110° F., and put into it about two cupfuls of **soap jelly**. Then let the machine run for two to three minutes to whip up a suds. If the solution seems to need more soap, add enough to produce a good, rich suds. Wash one blanket at a time if the blankets are double; if single, wash two together. Allow about fifteen minutes for the washing period, or longer if necessary, depending upon the amount of soil.

Blankets, like all woolen pieces, should never be wrung hard or twisted. Put them through the wringer, but release the tension of the rolls so that there is scarcely any pressure at all.

The wash water may look dark, but do not discard it, as it is still good as a dirt solvent and should all be removed in the rinsing. Instead, add more soap, work up a good suds, and use it to wash one more load of blankets.

LAUNDRY METHODS

The temperature of the rinse water should as nearly as possible approximate that of the wash water. Rinse as directed on page 182. Where you can be assured of a reasonably soft water for washing, better results are obtained by rinsing with clear water. The harder the water, however, the more essential will the soap rinse be found.

Bluing is both unnecessary and undesirable for blankets. They naturally have a creamy tint which is most attractive. I presuppose that you have selected a clear breezy day so that the drying will be rapid. **Quick drying** is almost the most important consideration in retaining the fluffy lightness of the new blanket. An ideal way is to spread them on a lawn with a sheet placed underneath to prevent any possibility of soil from grass or insects. If the blankets are spread over a line take pains to have the weight evenly distributed on either side. Be sure that edge and corners meet.

The **centrifugal dryer** is especially good for drying blankets since they develop a lightness and fluffiness like new, probably due to the rapidity with which the fabric was dried. But for those who have not such a drying method, the above directions will safeguard.

The same procedure in washing and rinsing can be used for down **quilts**. During the drying process, however, shake the quilts lightly every fifteen or twenty minutes if possible to redistribute the down. After the quilt is thoroughly dry the covering may be smoothed with a warm

BUSINESS OF HOUSEKEEPING

iron. Do not try to wash quilts filled with cotton or wool, but the latter may have their covers removed for washing and replaced when clean.

Fitting the Baby's Wash Into the House Routine

Every household is different in its plan of operation but so many single "maids of all work" look askance at a baby's wash, it occurred to me that some mothers would be interested in my handling of the situation.

First, whether you do it yourself or hire it done, see that all diapers and urine stained garments are given an immediate rinsing in cold water and in the toilet, which has been flushed to yield you plenty of fresh cold water. Cold water is a solvent for this type of stain and if this procedure is followed before the garment or diaper has been allowed to dry, you will have no trouble. Hot water, even warm water, adds to your difficulty by setting it as a stain.

Indeed if you once try my method I am sure you will be convinced of its ease and efficacy. I will guarantee that no diaper rash can appear through diapers thus handled.

After this first rinse wring as dry as possible and drop them into the diaper pail containing plenty of clear cold water. Once a day, preferably in the morning, they are washed in the laundry. In most cases they are run through the washing machine with a neutral soap solution, rinsed and hung to dry. In my case they were never boiled.

LAUNDRY METHODS

It may be heresy but try it as I did and be convinced. It is exceedingly bad practice to drop the diaper unrinsed into the diaper pail. Success depends upon making that first rinse a thorough one.

The **woolen shirts and bands** received their careful rinsing but were washed only twice a week. The same caution is needed with these. They must never be allowed to **dry** after urine or other discharge has stained them. If they should become dry they will require all of the drastic washing methods that are commonly used.

The **baby's bedding** changed twice a week, is best put into the regular wash from the start. If the sheets are wet, rinse in cold water and dry before sending to the laundry.

The **rubber sheet** is given a daily wash in plenty of cold not warm water. In this way the rubber sheet can be kept absolutely free of yellow stain if it is of the **woven stockinette type**. If of rubber the treatment will prolong its life of service. The tiny **slips and dresses** are washed by hand in the hand tub. They are ironed with the four-pound size of iron because it proves a bit more convenient to handle. It is quite possible to plan one of the twice-a-week wash days on the regular laundry day, leaving the other to fall on a Thursday, when presumably the laundry is free from its household burdens.

HOME-MADE SOAP FLAKES

If you live where it is impossible to get your favorite laundry soap in flake form, as I do now, try getting the bars of soap and running them through the food-grinder. The riper the soap, the easier it is to grind, but in any case grinding is easier than shaving with a knife and yields a flake that is very quickly dissolved. I grind several bars at a time and keep the flakes in a can until I want them, thus saving time on wash day.
—*Good Housekeeping Discovery.*

FOR COLORED EMBROIDERY PIECES

When dampening and rolling up any articles to be pressed that have colored embroideries or trimming, lay a piece of old white cloth between the colored portion and the surrounding material. This catches any slight fading or stain that might be transferred indelibly to the other part. I learned to do this after having an embroidered oyster pongee belonging to my little girl ruined by orange and blue stains from the hand work on it.
—*Good Housekeeping Discovery.*

WHEN WASHING LACE COLLARS

I have found that a cloth wrung out of thin starch water gives just enough stiffness to a lace collar to make it seem like new. Place the lace between two thicknesses of the cloth and iron until all are dry. The effect is soft but not "washed" looking.—*Good Housekeeping Discovery.*

LAUNDRY METHODS

ON IRONING DAY

On ironing days remember to slip a clean handkerchief into the pocket of each little garment, and the children will be ready with this often-forgotten article without having to think about it during the busy hour between breakfast and the start to school. Grown people also like to have things at hand, and if the links are put in the cuffs of soft shirts on the ironing table, they are not only ready to wear, but more easily folded.

—Good Housekeeping Discovery.

HANGING CLOTHES IN COLD WEATHER

In cold weather I place my clothes-pins in a pan in the warming oven. When I am ready to hang out the washing, I put the hot clothes-pins in the clothes-pin bag. Each time I reach for a pin, my fingers get warm, and the hot clothes-pins also help to keep the corners from freezing too much in hanging the clothes straight.

—Good Housekeeping Discovery.

KEEPING THE IRONING BOARD CLEAN

It is surprising how much dust can collect on an ironing board cover when it is not in use. To avoid just this very thing, I have made a cotton bag into which the ironing board can be slipped after each time of using. This bag is long enough to fold over at the top and thus protects the board from dirt and dust.

—Good Housekeeping Discovery.

DOLLS' CLOTHES-PINS SOLVE THE PROBLEM

Dolls' clothes-pins have proved very useful in hanging the baby's clothes on a cord across the upstairs piazza. The big pins fall out, and safety-pins are very apt to tear the clothes. —*Good Housekeeping Discovery.*

REMOVABLE COVERS FOR HOLDERS

I find ironing holders, and in fact all holders, are bound to get soiled when used for any great length of time, and it is not an easy task to wash and dry them when they are so thick. To ease the washing of the same, I make the foundation pads of the usual size and shape. Then I make slip-covers of the same size as the pads, having short tapes on the edges. These covers slip over the pads easily, being tied in position. When soiled, the covers alone are removed and washed. Gingham, percale, or something firm and washable is satisfactory for the covers.

—*Good Housekeeping Discovery.*

DRYING WOOLEN SWEATERS

Heavy woolen sweaters may be dried most successfully in the following way: Lay a clean sheet kept just for the purpose over a window screen. On this place the washed sweater in exactly its original form, carefully placing the fulness in the front, with a flat back. Balance the screen on two chairs and dry the sweater over a floor register or in a warm room in the winter time, or in a shady place out-of-doors if it is summer.

—*Good Housekeeping Discovery.*

Index

Account-keeping, 17
Adhesive Tape, new uses for, 58
Advertisements, newspaper and magazine, 94
Alcohol, denatured, uses for, 79
Ammonia, Household, 117
Aniline Bluing, for laundry, 153
Art Gum, uses for, 58
Attic, care of, 117
Awnings, care of, 115
Baby, washing for, 186
Banks, Home Service Departments of, 20
Bathroom, efficient, 50, 59
Bath Tub, brushes for, 57
Bed Spreads, 55
Bed Springs, 53
Beds, single, 52
Beds, and Bed Making, 51, 52
Blankets, 55; how to launder, 183; lengthening of, 55
Blotters, uses for, 77
Blues and Tints, for laundry, 152
Bluing, 179; aniline for laundry, 153; for laundry, 147; ultramarine for laundry, 152
Boiler, Copper for laundry, 142
Boiling, for certain garments, 164
Boiling Water, not essential for washing machines, 161
Bookcases, care of, 118
Books, care of, 118
Borax laundry soaps, 147
Bowls, mixing and cooking, 63
Breakfast, keeping coffee hot for, 33
Breakfast Table, 44
Brooms, ways to preserve, 33
Brushes, for bathtub, 57
Budgeting, 9, 17; a call to, 17; Envelope System, 18; helps for, 25; tables for dividing income, 20
Burners, types of, 82; wick type, 82; wickless type, 82
Carpet renovating, 119
Carpet Sweepers, 89
Carpets, 84
Carpets and Rugs, cleaning, 112, 113
Cabinet, Kitchen, 142
Cabinets, Wall, 130
Cellar, cleanliness of, 106; care of, 106; coal and wood bins, 107
Cement Floor, treatment of, 112; paint for, 136
Chambermaid-waitress, duties of, 37

Cheesecloth, uses for, 125
Chemicals for laundry, 144, 145; rules for their use, 171
Children's Rompers, how to launder, 164
China Closet, care of, 118
Cleaning, by electrolysis, 75; by vacuum, 119; metal, 78; rooms, 118
Closet, care of, 100, 102
Closet, Linen, care of, 101
Clothes, colored, how to launder, 169; men's, care of, 103; not to be soaped for laundry, 163; not to be soaked for laundry, 163
Clothes Chute, 131
Clothes-pins, doll's, uses for, 190
Clothes Posts, beautifying of, 133
Coal-bins, 109
Coal-range, care of, 81
Coat-hangers, for drying clothes, 146
Coffee, method for keeping hot, 33
Coffee Pot, how to clean, 64
Cold Storage, commercial, 100
Color, selection of, for floor, 86
Combs, how to clean, 58
Containers, metal, 123
Cook-Laundress, duties of, 37
Cooking Dishes, how to clean, 60
Cooking Utensils, care of, 80
Copper Boiler, for laundry, 142
Covers, washable, 113
Credit, buying on, 19, 23
Curtains, Cheesecloth, uses for, 125
Curtains and Portières, cleaning, 118
Dampness, prevention of, 123
Denatured Alcohol, uses for, 79
Dextrine, starch substitute, 158
Diapers, how to launder, 186
Dishpan, how to eliminate, 65
Dish-Towels, 66
Dishwasher, 12
Dishwashing, 60
Disinfectants, 117; Spraying Machines, 117
Down Pillows, 54
Downstairs, care of, 43, 45
Drainboard sink, 12
Dresser Mirror, 58
Dressing-table, 59
Dryer, electric centrifugal, 136
Dryer, quick for laundry, 130
Dryer Racks, 13
Dryers, 136; gas heated for laundry, 136; stove-heated for laundry, 136

191

INDEX

Drying Yard for Laundry, 131
Dutch Silver, cleaning of, 76
Dyes and Tints, for laundry work, 154
Electric Fuses, 124
Electric Lights, 77
Electricity, care in using, 77
Electrolysis Cleaning, 75
Embroidery Pieces, how to launder, 188
Envelope System, for accounts, 18
Equipment, Labor-saving, 9, 11; laundry, 13, 31, 129, 134; selection of, 13, 14
Expenses, how to itemize, 19, 20
Exterminator, Commercial, 105
Fabrics, colored, how to launder, 176
Fabrics, white, how to launder, 176
Family Wash, nature of soils of, 162; routine for, 165
Fats, animal, in family wash, 162
Faucet Attachments, 61
Faucets, 79; leaky, 21; nickeled, how cleaned, 79
Fire, prevention of, 123
Fireless Cookers, 12
Fireplaces, care of, 124
Firewood, 107
Flies, prevention of, 110
Floor, Cement, paint for, 134
Floors, care and treatment of, 84; Cement, treatment for, 112; colors for, 86; Hardwood, 91; how to clean, 91; Linoleum, 85; painted, 85; Porch, 112; shellacked, 89; soft wood, 91; tiling, 92; treatment and care of, 84; varnished, 85; washing of, 91; waxed, 87; wood, 85
"Fog," how to remove from furniture, 97
Food, purchase of, 22
Foods, perishable, 122
Formulas, washing, 147
Furnace, asbestos coverings for, 108; care of, 108; spring cleaning of, 108
Furniture, cleaning and polishing, 95; Lawn, 111; Overstuffed, cleaning of, 118; painted, 97; polishing of, 95; Porch, 111; renovating scratched, 49; Wicker and Reed, cleaning of, 97; Willow, 111
Furniture Polish, 111
Garments, Winter, storage of, 114
Gas Stove, 82
Georgette Crepes, how to launder, 179
German Silver, cleaning of, 76
Glassware, for Cooking, 80; how to clean, 62; washing of, 62
Good Housekeeping Savings Bank, 26
Good Housekeeping Institute, helps from, 14, 141
Grease Spots, how to remove, 46; on floor, 47

Gum Arabic, starch substitute, 158
Hampers, Laundry, 131
Hands, care of, 99
Hangings, Winter, 113
Hard Water, effects of, on laundry, 151
Heating, 22; how to reduce bills for, 22
Heating Leaks, 22
Heating Systems, water, 12
Help, schedule for, 29
Home Accounts, how kept, 20
House-cleaning, schedule for, 116; seasonal, 116
House, closing, procedure for, 120
Household Linen, how to launder, 164
Household Tasks, daily routine, 43; downstairs, 43; routine for, 41; Special, 71; upstairs, 50
Housekeepers and Servants, 27
Housekeeping, the new, 9; outdoor, 110; scientific, 15
Income, division of, 18, 20
Infants, washing for, 186
Ink Spots, how to remove from floor, 48
Insecticide, uses for, 115
Installment Plan, purchases by, 14
Iron, best weight for, 139
Iron, electric, cost of power, 140
Iron Rust, how to remove, 172
Ironer, open-end, 137
Ironing, 178; by hand, time study, 138; by machine, time study, 138
Ironing Board, suggestions for, 145
Ironing Boards, 13, 137
Ironing Day, 189
Ironing Machines, 31, 130, 136
Irons, Hand, 139
Irons, Electric, 139
Javelle Water, how to prepare, 171
Jewelry, care of, 122
Kitchen Cabinet, 11
Kitchen, cardboard for use in, 48
Kitchen Linoleum, 93
Kitchen Range, care of, 81
Kitchen Table, height of, 48
Kitchen and Laundry, combination of, 132
Labor-saving Equipment, 11
Lace Collars, how to launder, 188
Lamp Shades, silk, care of, 121
Lanoline, animal fat, 180
Laundry, plan and location, 129; aniline bluing for, 153; Blankets, 184; Baby's Wash, 186; Chemical Reagents for, 144; Diapers, 186; Embroidery pieces, 188; Equipment, 13, 134; Equipment, cost of, 130; essentials, 129; floor for, 134; Georgette crepes, 179; hampers for,

192

INDEX

131; how to sprinkle clothes, 173; how to wash silks, 176; how to wash white and colored pieces, 176; Javelle Water, 171; Lace Collars, 188; lighting of, 136; list of equipment for, 144, 145; Methods, 160; Oxalic Acid for, 171; Plain Soaps, 147; Potassium Permanganate for, 171; Routine for, 166; six essential facts concerning, 163; Stockings to be washed separately, 169; Tools, 132; Ultramarine Bluing for, 152; washing of underwear, 164; water hardness affecting, 151; water softening for, 151; Woolens, 180; walls for, 134; wiring of, 135
Laundry Soaps, 147; borax, 147; naphtha, 147; plain, 147
Laundry Spoons, 132
Laundry Starch, 156
Laundry Trays, 140
Laundry and Kitchen, combination of, 132
Lemon Juice, for hands, 99
Lemon Rinds, uses for, 83
Lighting, 21; how to reduce bills for, 21
Lighting Fixtures, care of, 122
Linen, 51
Linen Closet, care of, 101
Lingerie Tints and Dyes, 154
Lining-paper, 117
Linoleum, 13; for flooring, 112; kitchen, 93; laying of, 93
Liquid Wax, 89
Living-Room, 45
Locks, care of, 124
Machine, Ironing, 136
Machine, Washing, 140
Magazine Advertisements, 94
Maid, single, régime for, 29; duties of, 29, 30
Maids, schedule for two, 37, 38
Matches, danger of, from mice, 123; safeguarding, 123
Mattress, selection of, 54
Mattress Pad, 56
Men's Clothes, care of, 103
Metal, cleaning of, 78
Metal Containers, 123
Mildew, how to remove, 173, 175
Mirrors, 58
Monthly Payment System, 19
Mop, Dish, how to dry, 66
Mops, Floor, 52; oil polish, 88; Chemical Dust, 89
Moth Prevention, 120
Moth Preventives, 117
Moth-proof Bags, 103
Moth-proof Chests, 117
Moths, fumigation for, 105; protection against, 114

Naphtha Soaps, 147; for use with hard water, 151
Neckbands, how to launder, 31
Newspaper Advertisements, 94
Oil-polish Mop, 88
Oil Stove, 82
Open-end Ironer, 137
Overcoats and Suits, care of, 104
Oxalic Acid, how to prepare, 171
Padded Polisher, use of, 88
Pans, roasting, cleaning, 63
Papered Walls, how cleaned, 97
"Piece bags," 103
Pillows, 54
Polish, Furniture, 111
Polish Mop, use of, 89
Polishing Cloths, for silver, 74
Portières, cleaning of, 118
Potassium Permanganate, how to prepare, 171
Prussian Blue, 152
Quilts, Down, 185
Radiators, how to clean, 119
Rain water, for laundry, 149
Range, Kitchen, care of, 81
Refrigeration, Electric, 12
Refrigerator, care of, 67; cleaning of, 67; how to clean, 68
Renovating, Spring, 110
Room Cleaning, 118
Rugs, cleaning of, 118
Rugs and Carpets, cleaning, 112, 113
Sales, advantages of, 24; department store, 24
Sandpaper, uses for, 94
Saucepans, how to clean, 63
Savings Bank, 26
Savings, how to accumulate, 20, 21
Screens, care of, 110
Screens, Window, care of, 98
Scrap-Book, for household furnishings, 94
Sewing-machine, Electric, 13
Sewing-table, 142
Servant, single, 29; weekly schedule for, 27
Servants and Housekeepers, 27
Servants, care of, 34; engagement of, 36; Régime for two, 34; Routine for two, 34, 35; working schedules for, 38
Sheets, size of, 83
Sheets and Blankets, 55
Shellac, uses of, 112; for cement floors, 112
Shoe Carrier, 102
Shoes, care of, 102
Shopping, 23, 24
Silk, rules for laundering, 176
Silks, how to launder, 169, 176

INDEX

Silver, care of, 122; cleaning of, 73; how to clean, 73, 74; polishing cloth for, 74
Silver and China, how to wash, 60
Sink Drainer, 60
Soap, castile, 95
Soap Chips, 147
Soap Flakes for Laundry work, 155
Soap Flakes, home-made, 188
Soap, how to utilize scraps, 39
Soap, in solution, 148
Soap Jelly, uses of, 155
Soap-shaker, new use for, 146
Soap-tints, 154
Soaps and Soap Compounds, 147; borax, 147; dye for laundry work, 155; for laundry purposes, 181; flake and powdered, 148; naphtha, 148; to be used in solutions, 163
Soft Water, effects of, on laundry, 149
Solutions, washing, 166, 167
Sponges, Rubber, 59
Spoons, Laundry, 132
Spraying Machines, for disinfectants, 117
Spring Renovating, 110
Stains, their reagents, 172; Chocolate, 172; Coffee and Tea, 172; Fruit, 172; Grass, 172; how to remove, 170; Ink, 172; Iron Rust, 172; Mildew, 172; Tea and Coffee, 172; Vaseline, 173; Wagon Grease, 173
Starch, formulas, 156; substitutes, 158; and Starching, 156; varieties of, 159
Starching clothes, 159
Stockings, to be washed separately, 169
Storage Problems, 103
Storeroom, care of, 100
Storeroom, protection of against mice and rats, 107
Storm Windows and Doors, 110
Sotve, Gas, 82
Stove, Kitchen, care of, 81
Stove, Oil, 82
Strength, conservation of, 15
"Suds" for laundry, 150
Suits and Overcoats, care of, 104
Supplies, Food, 24; staple, 24
Surfaces, woodwork, cleaning of, 98
Sweaters, woolen, how to dry, 190
Table, Kitchen, height of, 48
Table Pad, 32
Tape, adhesive, 58
Tea Pot, how to clean, 64
Telephone, long distance calls, timing of, 33; ordering by, 23
Thermos Bottle, uses for, 33
Tints and Blues for laundry, 152

Tints and Dyes for laundry work, 154
Toilet seats, cleaning of, 92
Tool Room, 107
Transoms, for Ventilation, 135
Traps, care of, 124
Turpentine, uses for 88, 112
Ultramarine Bluing, for laundry, 152
Underwear, how to launder, 164
Upstairs, care of, 50
Vacuum Cleaner, 13, 88, 104
Vacuum Cleaning, 119
Varnish, hard waterproof, 135
Varnish stains, how to mix, 86
Vaseline, how to remove stain, 173
Vases, flower, 45; silver, 45
Ventilation, 135
Wagon Grease, how to remove stain, 173
Waitress-chambermaid, duties of, 37
Wall Cabinets, 130
Wall, surfaces, cleaning of, 98
Walls, papered, care of, 97
Wash, Family, routine for, 165
Wash, sanitary, without boiling, 165
Washing, chemistry of, 160
Washing Formulas, 147, 151
Washing Machine, 31, 129, 166, 179
Washing Machines, how to use, 166, 167; piping of, 141
Washing Soda, 149
Washing Solutions, 166, 167
Water, rain, for laundry, 149
Water Hardness, affecting laundry work, 151
Water Softeners, for laundry, 149
Water Softening Plants for laundry, 151
Wax, for floors, 87
Wax, liquid, 89; how to apply, 90
Wax, paste, uses for, 112
Wax Polish, liquid, 111
Weekly Schedule, for servant, 31
White Clothes, washing of, 168
Whitewashing, uses for, 109
Window Screens, care of, 98
Women's Clothes, care of, 102, 103
Woodwork surfaces, cleaning of, 98
Wool Blankets, care of, 103
Woolen Sweaters, how to launder, 190
Woolens, how to launder, 180
Wools, how to launder, 169; how to dry after washing, 182
Work Bench, for laundry, 143
Window Shades, how to attach, 32; renewing of, 99
Winter Garments, care of, 114
Wiring, for lighting, 135
Wristbands and Neckbands, how to launder, 162